MENTORING

MENTORING

A Practical Guide to the Skills of Mentoring

Reg Hamilton

Published in 2003 by
Spiro Press
17-19 Rochester Row
London SW1P 1LA
Telephone: +44 (0)870 400 1000

ISBN 1 84439 008 X

First published by The Industrial Society 1993

Reprinted: 1994, 1995, 1996, 1999, 2001, 2003

Ref: 6197.JC.1.2003

British Library Cataloguing-in-Publication Data.
A catalogue record for this book is available from the British Library.

Spiro Press USA
3 Front Street, Suite 331
PO Box 338
Rollinsford NH 03869
USA

Typeset by: Photoprint, Torquay, Devon
Printed by: Formara
Text illustrations: Sophie Grillet

Acknowledgements

This book is dedicated to three of my mentors
without whom it would probably not have been written:

Paul Harvey who made it important,
Gerald O'Callaghan who made it possible,
and Sheridan Maguire who made it a pleasure.

Contents

List of Figures

List of Tables

1 What is Mentoring?

Introduction

If you are thinking about becoming someone's mentor or even if you have already started doing the job, you may have been asking yourself: what kind of person makes a **good** mentor and what **exactly** does it involve?

Reading this chapter will answer these questions and reading the book will provide comprehensive guidance on how to be effective in the role.

This book provides a step by step guide to the important skills a mentor requires, in order to enhance and accelerate the learning of those placed under her or his care.

One difficulty in answering the question 'What is mentoring?' is that the word has a rather different meaning for different people. BP Chemicals state in their *Mentor's*

Manual that 'Mentoring creates a particular, personal relationship within a general framework of developing and managing Company newcomers'. Most advocates of mentoring as a development tool see the mentor as a 'non-judgmental friend'. There are mentoring schemes which involve mentors in assessing and reporting on their learners but my own view is that these all lose some of their developmental potential, because the relationship between mentor and learner is not as relaxed nor as rich as it could be. A 1992 conference of educators attended by representatives from the industrial and commercial world, spent a good deal of time debating this point and disagreeing about what kind of people mentors were and what they should or should not do.

Changes in the method of training teachers prompted this conference and the fact that a number of academic institutes had adopted the term 'mentor' to describe the role of college based staff who visit trainee teachers in order to advise and **assess** them. Some at the conference thought it a better term for the teachers, who assist and **assess** the college students or 'licensed trainees' work, during the time they spend in their classroom.

The Engineering Institutes have also renamed their trainer/ tutors, as a way of signalling a change of emphasis in their approach to professional development. These Institutes use the word 'mentor' to describe those members who, in addition to being a resource to those seeking chartered status, **monitor the experience and certify** that a (usually young) engineer has had an approved range of responsibilities since graduating and is suitable to become a member of the Institute.

Listening to members of different professions using the term it can seem that one has slipped into Lewis Carroll's world of Humpty Dumpty where a word can mean

*'. . . just what I choose it to mean – neither more nor less'.**

The situation is no better when we look at what mentors do. Many managers will recognise the actions, responsibilities and skills associated with the mentor role and claim that they use those skills and take those actions. They are right. The only real difference in the two roles lies in the nature and focus of responsibility. Managers are paid to get results and developing their staff contributes to achieving that goal. The mentor's sole point of focus is the development of her/his learner as shown in Figure 1.

This development by the mentor occurs 'as required' rather than in the formal, organised way of the academic world or work-related courses and workshops, where everything is taken in a logical order.

The mentor speeds up the process of integration into a new organisation or work role, by ensuring that the learner derives maximum benefit from their new experience. Typically they help the trainee to understand how things get done within their new job and how to best use their own strengths in influencing events. To use a piece of jargon it is *learner-centred not curriculum driven.* In simple terms people learn at a pace which matches their experience, not in some order determined by theory.

* p242 *Alice's Adventures in Wonderland and Through the Looking Glass* – William Clowes & Sons Ltd.

RESPONSIBILITIES

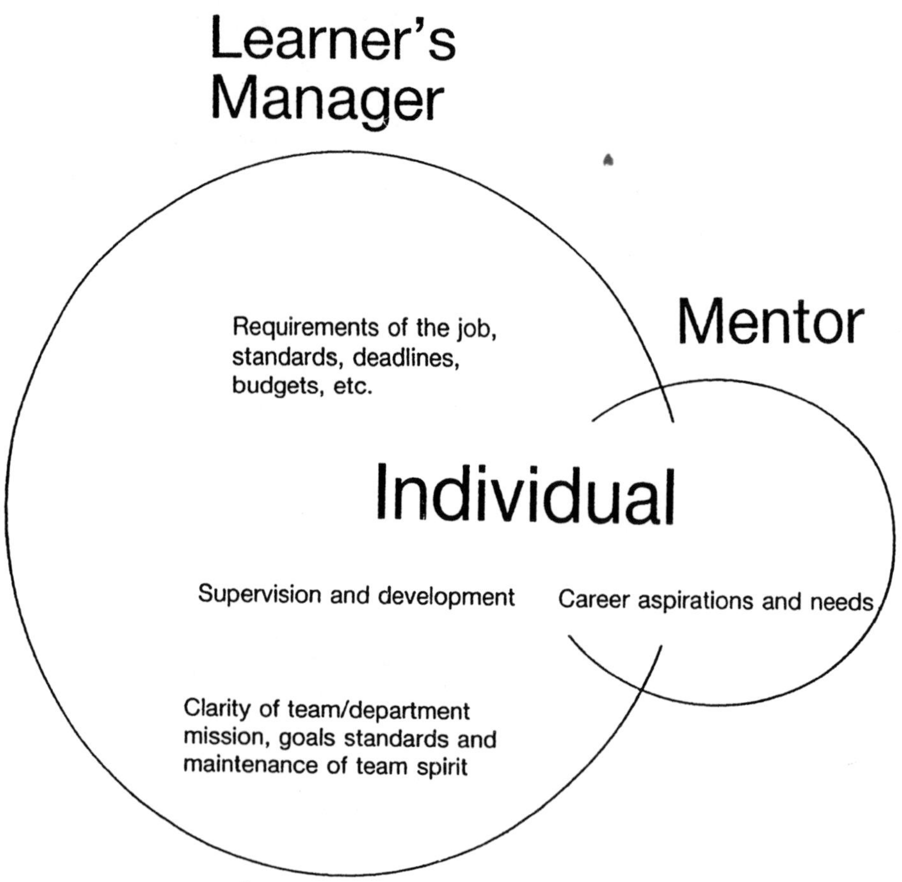

Fig. 1 Manager–Mentor Responsibility

Mentors use some of the skills of the manager to develop the person they are helping (see Figure 2). This overlap is one cause of the conflict alluded to above, the range of mentoring schemes used by organisations is another.

Given this confusion it may be best to give some background and then describe a number of the formal approaches to mentoring, the purposes they serve, and their potential benefits and difficulties. This will highlight that debates about whether one approach to mentoring is right and another wrong, are pointless. The differences between them are due to the fact that they serve different purposes and therefore, inevitably, demands upon mentors differ.

Background

Mentoring is as old as history. The *Shorter Oxford Dictionary* states that the word is Greek in origin. It has connections with *'to remember, think, counsel'*. In the modern world the idea probably originated in this country but has been developed more fully (like assessment centres), in the USA.

In America it appears to have received a boost from their Equal Employment Opportunities legislation. Many companies, wanted to change their management profile to include females, blacks and other minorities so that they remained eligible for government contracts. Historically, white males had succeeded and they held most of the middle and senior management jobs. It was recognised that 'minority' employees faced problems, in part, because they had a low opinion of themselves and lacked suitable role-models. Training programmes alone would not address

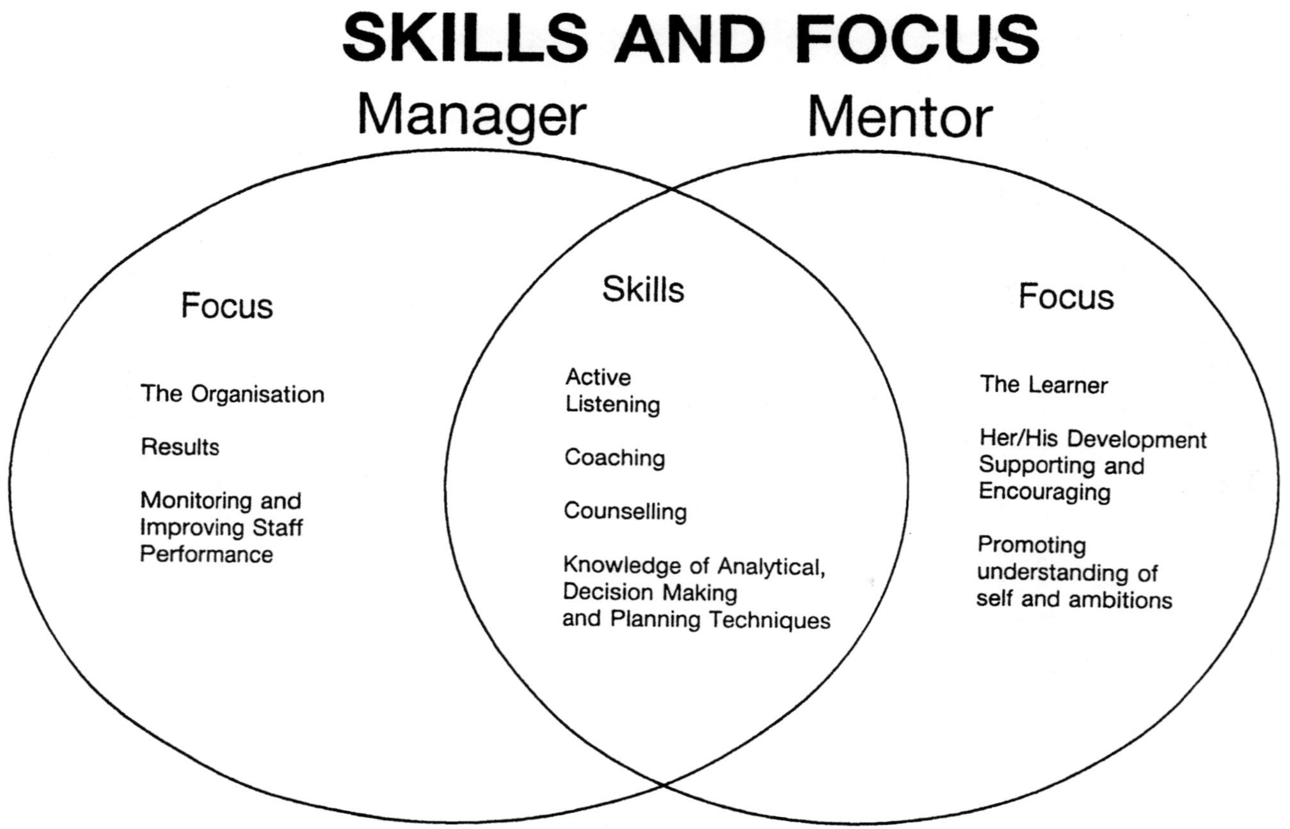

Fig. 2 Manager–Mentor Skills Overlap and Difference in Focus

these issues, a comprehensive coaching and support system was required.

In the UK, companies like British Airways and BP, faced with a temporary shortage of management talent or the desire to improve the quality of some of their training, also turned to mentoring. But it goes back further than that. British family businesses established in the last century ensured their continuity by 'grooming' those offspring who showed an interest in, and aptitude for, the business. Cadbury's, McVitie's (United Biscuits) and other household names, may have flourished not only because, as a 1992 survey showed, they are able to take a long term view in their investment policies, but also because they have provided mentors for their chief executives of the future.

Informal mentoring has always gone on, of course, and will continue. It happens when someone finds they can readily relate to, and confide in, a more experienced employee or manager they admire. It need not even be someone from work, provided that the mentor has a genuine interest in the growth and development of the person concerned. It will, of course, work best if they also have the necessary skills and personal qualities to increase her or his confidence and competence.

Some mentoring relationships begin when senior people take an interest in, and promote the cause of, a subordinate or person they believe has untapped potential. Some people actively seek a mentor and approach another to help them learn. The result is that the UK now has a wide range of approaches to mentoring, each with its own aims and consequent demands on mentors' experience and skills.

Approaches to Mentoring

The range of approaches to mentoring found in this country is partly because organisations have not always clearly identified their precise aims. The result is that mentors sometimes lack clear guidelines and are not adequately selected or trained. The descriptions which follow are given in their 'pure' form, as if the world were a simple place in which discrete boundaries can be readily drawn. In reality, some organisations have combined two or more of these approaches.

The '*Sponsor*' System

Mentors in this situation can look as though they have a magic wand in the way that they sponsor their learners. They provide a wide variety of experience through special projects and assignments. They effect introductions to key figures in the organisation and ensure that their learner's achievements are recognised widely, by giving them 'high-exposure' projects and tasks to do. These mentors may challenge, confront, cajole and coach because they have a stake in the individual and may lose face if s/he should fail.

The primary aim is to develop an individual or small élite group very quickly, in order to meet known short-term needs identified by Management Succession planning to ensure that these 'talented' people do not leave the organisation.

The mentor in these cases is a mature, senior manager, (board level in many companies), with influence, power and credibility. They may not have had formal training in coaching, counselling or other interpersonal skills. On the other hand, few can have progressed to senior level without some ability in these areas. My own recommendation, based upon what learners say about their very varied skill, is that they should receive appropriate training. The relationship is probably more successful when the learner can speak frankly and this does require specific skills and attitudes on the mentor's part. Where the learner has felt free to challenge or confront their mentor on current issues, this has been reported as a benefit by both learner and mentor. One mentor was shocked to hear that a new employee development programme was seen as 'Management opting out' and as part of a recent cost-cutting exercise. The new approach was more expensive, but potentially more effective than the old. The senior manager was unaware of current scepticism and how lamentably management had failed to communicate and convince employees of the long-term benefits of the previous changes.

Mentors say that they enjoy having someone, to 'think out loud with', who provides a unique perspective on a proposal. This approach to mentoring can retain talent and allow the organisation to fully use the capabilities of individuals, at the earliest time possible. However, it can result in those being mentored having unrealistic expectations about their prospects. It can also arouse envy, antagonism, and low motivation amongst those not selected to be part of this exclusive group. It may cause the organisation to lose people who make a valuable contribution and the odd 'star' who develops late and subsequently 'shines' elsewhere.

Peer Group Mentoring

There are a variety of approaches to peer group mentoring, whose aims and methods vary according to their target population. Most common is newly recruited staff, but there are many examples, in the National Health Service and elsewhere, involving more mature staff. In the case of new recruits, the mentoring system attempts to provide them with a responsible and well-informed friend and to introduce management skills to the young people appointed as mentors.

These mentors, at the pre-management stage of their careers, have 2–3 years experience, a positive attitude towards their job and organisation and are seen as managers of the future. A selected group are taught assertiveness, coaching, counselling and other skills they will require in order to be effective when they are managers. Those suitable are then selected as mentors and given further specific training to equip them for the mentor role.

They are selected for their maturity, early potential for management and inter-personal skills. In addition to training in the skills required, they meet regularly with other mentors. This review/continuous development process ensures that they receive any further training and advice required and never feel isolated or unsupported.

An important benefit of this approach is that the training potential mentors receive, is essential to their eventual effectiveness as managers. More importantly, they get the chance to practice these skills in relatively low risk situations as someone's 'organisational friend', not their manager. The learners benefit from having someone allocated to them who is likely to share many of their interests and values, because there is no 'generation gap' as there can be when mentors are more experienced staff or managers.

It does require substantial support and good administrative systems to monitor quality, because of the comparative inexperience of the mentors. Like the first approach described, it can also result in people having unrealistic expectations. In this case, those chosen as mentors can have delusions about how close they are to becoming managers.

Some organisations using this approach provide a 'mentoring supervisor' who provides an ear, in confidence, and may advise on how to deal with any difficulties met by the learner, which the mentor cannot resolve.

Formal peer group mentoring to develop mature staff who are changing jobs is mostly found, at present, where there is a degree of complexity to the change; for example, a female appointed to a level at which she will be the only one of her sex, or someone crossing professional lines like a scientist moving into finance or human resources. People without much formal education, promoted to management because of their technical expertise or experience, sometimes have a mentor to help with day-to-day aspects of management. It is often the case that these people learn more effectively if they receive practical help, as the need arises, rather than attend training courses.

This is, in my view, one of the great untapped areas of mentoring. Small companies, or those with restricted budgets in particular, could make much more use of their resources if they selected, trained and used mentors to develop others. The recent interest in the 'Learning Organisation' as written about by Dr Mike Pedler and his colleagues may help to speed the process.

When used with mature staff, this approach does not seem to have the disadvantages of other schemes already mentioned. It can enlarge the job of those chosen as mentors and increase the motivation of good performers at all levels of the organisation, without having élitist connotations.

Self-Development Mentoring

This approach is used to demonstrate to young people the responsibility they have for making use of the development opportunities the employer provides. The aim is to ensure that people recruited are proactive, self-confident, action-oriented employees, who will, in time, become competent managers. Organisations attempting major restructuring or culture change are increasingly supplementing their efforts in this way and a similar approach can be found in those using 'Action Learning' groups, or sponsoring employees on MBA (Master Degree in Business Administration) or similar programmes.

The preparation often starts with an action-oriented week of training. Participants are encouraged to learn more about themselves and each other through a series of questionnaires, group and individual exercises. They learn how to learn, are introduced to the 'Experiential Learning Cycle' described in the next chapter and develop inter-personal skills like assertion, coaching, counselling, giving and receiving feedback designed to help them be a resource to others. The overall objective is to form the entire group of trainees into an autonomous learning community. They are encouraged to identify strengths and resources within their ranks and to use these by keeping in touch with each other on a regular basis.

This system works best if the mutual cooperation fostered is kept under review. This was done with great success in one British Airways scheme, where trainees kept in touch on a regular basis through their study supervisor. They would meet and advise each other on how best to 'enter' and learn effectively in a particular department in which they had already been. Even if they had no experience in a department a colleague was destined to join, they would discuss what they had learned thus far in an attempt to maximise each other's learning.

In addition, the entire group met at regular intervals for specific training like report writing, or with their mentors. This may have worked as well as it did because the mentors had joined their learners for parts of their 'self-development' training.

The British Airways mentors in this scheme were young, upwardly mobile managers for whom the responsibility, training and experience of mentoring was likely to have a maturing, beneficial effect. Those selected had the reputation of being good people managers and were given counselling skills training.

These trainees were a mixture of internal and external recruits ranging from people relatively fresh from university, banking and other professions to those with little formal education, but wide experience of the airline over as much as ten years. They had a lot to offer each other but are unlikely to have done so under any conventional training scheme. It was, in effect, a two tier mentoring system, in that each person in addition to their appointed mentor treated others as mentors, often using different individuals in varying circumstances.

Ideally 'self-development' mentors should have counselling and other inter-personal skills but these can be developed 'on the job' given the programme's emphasis on self-reliance and the fact that trainees do have their peers as resources.

One of the major benefits of this approach is that it promotes the independence and self-determination espoused by so many modern organisations It can also prove a powerful instrument of culture change, because of the demands for changed behaviour it makes on managers used to directing events and exercising control. However, this pressure for wide-scale change can be its undoing. It is costly and time consuming to train managers to cope with these new demands made upon them and put in place the support systems necessary to maintain the change. The potential benefits are enormous, but they go to the organisation that has a clear vision of a desired future, a sustainable long-term strategy and a senior management team that can battle its way through the early difficulties.

Managers as Mentors

Some purists (those who criticise the use of the term mentor in teaching and the engineering professions), would argue that this is not really an approach to mentoring at all but simply a change of emphasis in the line manager's role.

One company used this approach to improve induction of newly recruited MBAs and introduce them to the company culture. The trainees varied from young graduates who had gone straight on to obtain their MBA, to those who had decided upon a mid-career change. These trainees were placed in the care of experienced, loyal managers of long service. The company had a 'Staff Development Committee' which was responsible for overseeing the career development of all employees with potential for rapid development and this committee regularly discussed each person's progress with his or her mentor. However, a secondary aim of this and similar schemes is to remotivate and enrich the job of 'plateauxed' managers by emphasising the key role they can play in developing the organisation's newly recruited talent.

The organisation which used this approach for MBAs, provided a one-week programme of training to potential mentors covering subjects of central importance to the company's culture and strategic plans, so that they could speak with confidence and authority. They also received information on learning and a range of mentoring skills and were then given the opportunity to opt out. Two of the first course did so.

The programme received high profile support from senior managers who visited for a formal dinner and spoke about their personal perspective on the company's long-term plans and how the mentor's role fitted into these. Other helpful factors in this company were its 'strong' culture, tradition of life-long employment and good record on training.

Typically trainees are in a department for a specific time period doing a real job of work, but mentor/managers know the aim is to integrate and develop them. As a result the trainee receives a high proportion of the manager's time and attention. It is not a conventional mentor role because, as managers, they report on all aspects of the learners' performance and development and do not develop the 'personal' relationship which usually occurs between mentor and learner.

The mentors were amongst the first to experience any new training and were regularly involved in discussion of other subjects relevant to their mentor role. They enjoyed their greater contact with senior managers and some have found that their own careers started to revive, as the way they saw themselves and how they were viewed by senior managers, changed through their involvement in mentoring and the 'Staff Development Meetings.'

These mentors were chosen for their track record of developing staff, their stability in their role, their maturity, balanced judgement and their loyalty. They were competent in giving feedback, coaching, counselling and other inter-personal skills.

One of the major difficulties these managers, and the organisations using this approach, face, is coping with resentment from other employees. For this reason it is likely to work best in particular cultures and requires careful choice of the specific jobs and departments in which the new recruits are placed.

On the other hand I detect that large multi-national companies under-going rapid re-organisation and change are seeking ways to make this approach work. The high mobility of their management, flatter hierarchy and desire for employees to take more initiative make it a highly suitable strategy.

Role Model

Any mentor is inevitably a role model for their mentee; the nature of the relationship ensures this, even if it is not a planned part of the scheme. The mentor's attitudes, values, problem solving strategies and general approach to life, as well as how s/he treats the learner and others, are all information to the learner. They will not copy these mindlessly but they will be influenced by this behaviour.

Table 1 APPROACHES TO MENTORING

MENTOR PROFILE	SPONSOR	PEER GROUP	SELF DEVELOPMENT	MANAGER	ROLE MODEL	INFORMAL
STATUS	Senior Manager often Board level.	Within one or two 'job grades' of learner. Comparable in age	'Official' mentors usually have a minimum of two years' management experience. (Fellow self-developers also act as mentors)	Varies but usually has minimum of 2 years' experience as a manager.	Variable but with a history of success in their field.	Variable but existing in the eyes of the learner.
EXPERIENCE	Long and varied.	1. Mentoring new recruits: two or three years service with the employer. 2. Mature learners: a history of success in the type of job learner is moving into.	See above	Likely to have had line rather than specialist experience with responsibility for managing people.	Variable but relevant to the learner's needs.	Variable but either relevant to learner's needs or mentor is skilled counsellor.
QUALITIES	Powerful and influential – able to make things happen.	Mature, self-confident, and well balanced individuals able to relate easily and understand others.	Positive, upwardly mobile managers	Well-motivated and well adjusted person with a history of relating well to junior employees and aiding their development.	Mature well adjusted individual with a genuine desire to help newcomers to their profession/occupation	Over-riding quality is interest in and commitment to learner's continued growth and development.

SKILLS	Listening, Strategic Thinking, Networking, Open to and able to build upon new ideas.	Coaching, Counselling, Assertion, Group Dynamics, Learning and Motivation	As for peer group mentor	As for peer group mentor.	Coaching, Counselling, etc	Relevant in eyes of mentor and learner.
SPECIAL TRAINING	None essential but thorough briefing and reminder on coaching and counselling recommended.	1. Usually a series of two day modules on key management skills above. Followed by Mentor training. 2. Often none but one or two days advised.	Mentors – 2 day counselling course and 2 × 1 day mentor briefing/training. Trainees – varies from one to ten days as required.	Varies from 1 or 2 day briefing/ mentor training to series of workshops on Coaching, Counselling, Learning etc according to need.	Residential course for students. Short initial briefing/ training for mentors.	None
OTHER SUPPORT	Given gap in age, status, and experience between mentor and protégé a mentoring coordinator or other 'intermediary' is recommended, (often a Training Department duty)	1. Young mentors often have a 'Mentor's Supervisor' – a resource in case of need and regular peer group meetings. 2. Regular peer reviews with other mentors recommended.	Self-Development tutor/facilitator acts as resource to both trainees and mentors	Regular meetings/ training with other mentors and Mentoring administrator or 'Champion'.	Regular meetings with Student Liaison Officer.	Mentor may make extensive use of own network.

Many employers in this country have lagged behind their US counterparts in the efforts they have made to accelerate the growth of their 'minority' employees. However Afro-Caribbean groups, in particular, are recognising the value of mentoring and the importance of positive role models. One London scheme matches students from a variety of ethnic backgrounds, with non-indigenous mentors who have a history of success in the field the student hopes to enter. Both mentors and mentees complete application forms indicating what they have to offer/require and a student liaison officer matches them. The scheme is strongly student driven; they specify whether they are looking for someone to help them deal with personal issues, provide relevant work experience, or guide them in their academic work, etc.

Both mentors and students receive training designed to help them make the best of the relationship and mentors meet regularly for further training/discussion with the student liaison officer. Some of these meetings are attended by mentees as the scheme calls them.

This is not a complete list of approaches to mentoring. It is quite common for two or more of the approaches described above to be combined. For example, organisations using some form of Action Learning, based upon Professor Reg Revans' approach to development, often use a combination of *Peer Group* and *Self-Development Mentoring*, as part of their support system for learners, without ever using the term mentor. If you are already involved in mentoring you may feel that your employer's approach has not been mentioned, but you may recognise elements of your scheme in the summary table.

Like the review of approaches which preceded it, this table is not comprehensive and does not cover all the approaches to mentoring to be found in UK. For example, it does not show the approach (mentioned in the text above), in which managers are asked to mentor a new recruit in their department, but it shows the more common example of managers being asked to mentor someone in another department. However, I do believe that any scheme in existence is likely to comprise a combination of the features shown above under one or other of the headings in the table.

Summary

Mentoring is a way of helping another understand more fully, and learn more comprehensively from, their day-to-day experience. It works best when it is a confidential relationship, which gives the learner the opportunity to speak freely about any concerns they may have. The range of skills and other qualities required by mentors will vary according to the objectives of mentoring and the way in which the organisation concerned has chosen to meet them.

This chapter has indicated some of the features to be found in UK approaches to mentoring, but it has not discussed any of the pitfalls hinted at throughout. Chapter 2 deals with some of these issues and describes how some organisations have tackled the difficulties encountered. It also gives guidance on how to get started as a mentor which will be helpful, whether you are involved in a formal approach to mentoring or simply helping with the development of someone whose interests you have at heart.

Note

The confusion about the mentor's role discussed in this chapter is matched by the disagreement on what those they are helping should be called. (This is discussed more fully on p.26.) Unless there is a particular reason for using *protégé* or *mentee* the term *learner* has been used throughout the book.

2

What Do Mentors Do?

Introduction

This chapter focuses on the important part that mentors play in ensuring that learners gain all they can from their early experience in their new role. The 'learning from experience cycle' is used as a way of exploring the behaviours and skills that mentors require to enhance learning in this way. Finally, it discusses the difficulty that some organisations have in convincing line managers of the need for a mentor scheme and the strategies that have been adopted to overcome this resistance.

All of the schemes described in Chapter 1 with the exception of **Role Model** and **Informal Mentoring,** are attempts to improve the quality of learning which occurs as someone does their day-to-day job. Even with teachers completing an academic-based course, the focus of the mentor is on what the students do during their 'teaching practices', not upon their academic assignments dealing with theoretical issues. In commercial and other institutions this 'on the job' development has always been the province of the line manager, the learner's boss.

There have been, over the years, a number of attempts to improve this 'on the job' training (Skills Analysis; Training Within Industry [TWI], etc., but the focus of each has been on the person doing the instruction. All have been attempts to have the instructor understand more about the learning process and teach them how to organise their instruction in a way which makes it easier for the learner to learn. It seems that the over-riding model of each of them was 'learner as empty vessel which has to be filled'. The other consistent thread in all of them was the clear responsibility of the 'boss' to identify what employees should know, or be able to do, and to ensure that gaps in knowledge and skill were filled.

The introduction of a formal mentoring scheme does not change this responsibility in any way; it simply places learners more in the centre of the learning process. It helps them to improve their ability to learn, rather than trying to improve the supervisor's ability to teach. It is not an alternative to what has been done in the past, as much as an additional aid to managers responsible for developing their staff.

This is not readily understood by line managers and many organisations which have introduced mentoring have had to deal with anxiety and hostility on the part of managers. They have feared that mentors were taking on some of their responsibilities and undermining their authority. Sometimes directors and other senior staff also need to be persuaded that the introduction of mentors is not a criticism of their managers and their ability to relate to and manage staff appropriately. The reality of most organisations is that many managers are skilled in fostering the development of those who report to them but some are not.

BP Chemicals carried out a series of surveys of graduates with up to two years service and identified that many line managers were too engrossed in their other responsibilities to develop new staff as rapidly and as well as was required. Another large commercial organisation discovered through comprehensive exit interviews, that leavers had felt insufficiently challenged or supported during their early months in a new job, even if they had worked for the organisation for some time. This evidence obviously helped to prove that there was a need and that the problem of anxiety and hostility from managers had to be overcome.

These anxieties and difficulties arise because of the similarity between the duties and responsibilities of a mentor and the responsibility any manager has for developing employees. The difference lies in the focus and emphasis that each have in carrying out their specific duties in relation to the person they are supervising (manager), or helping (mentor).

Managers can never step back from their responsibility for achieving results. Any action they take has as its back-drop the fact that their performance will be judged (and their career may be affected), by the effectiveness of their department and the efficiency of their staff. Mentors can be much more limited in their focus because their sole responsibility is the development of their learner or protégé.*

This difference in responsibility and emphasis explains why it is difficult for a manager to be a truly effective mentor to a member of her or his staff and why the mentor–learner relationship works best when it is truly confidential.

Employees know that their manager's opinion is important to their careers and that how they are judged by their managers could be affected not only by how they perform but also by what s/he knows about them. The result is a measure of reserve between boss and subordinate that is not found in successful mentor–protégé relationships. People find it easier to admit that they do not know something or face up to errors when they are with a *non-judgmental friend*.

Dealing effectively with a learner's misgivings and concerns about their performance, so that the result is increased confidence and effective strategies for improvement, is the essence of the mentor's role; it is **how** they help. To meet

* Some readers may object to this term and some organisations avoid it. Some use the word *learner* or they substitute an invented word *mentee*. The difficulty that people have with the word protégé is to do with a fear that it implies an attempt to clone, in their own image, those they are mentoring or to turn out some idealised model employee. Sometimes objectors to the term protégé can sound as if they are confusing **Acolyte**, which is defined as: *an attendant; a devoted follower*, with **Protégé**, which The Shorter Oxford English Dictionary defines as: *One who is under the protection or care of another*. The word learner is used throughout this book to avoid any confusion.

this primary responsibility for ensuring that learners make the best possible use of their experience, mentors need to know what learners are doing within the organisation and help them to make links between this new experience and their previous knowledge so that they recognise its relevance to their future.

When mentors succeed in doing this they improve their learner's morale, enhance their self-esteem and make their transition into their new role more speedy and less painful for them. The organisation benefits by having fewer failures in new jobs and by being able to move young people into responsible positions earlier in their careers. Mentors report that the satisfaction they receive from facilitating someone's growth in this way, is much greater than they would receive from teaching them, or simply telling them what to do.

In accomplishing this, mentors use a variety of skills as they take the person they are helping through the 'learning by experience' cycle. The idea that there are specific stages in the process of learning by experience was first described by Kolb, Rubin & McIntyre in 1974. They said that in the modern world and in a period of rapid change, we need to think of learning in the same way as we think about problem solving; not as something abstract which only occurs in special settings (school, etc), or circumstances (training courses), but as something which is central and relevant to our everyday lives.

Their view is that there is a four-stage cycle which we all go through (consciously or unconsciously), whenever we make good use of any new experience. The whole process starts when we do something, provided that as we take that action, we are aware of what is happening and have the ability to reflect upon it (Stage 2). In order for the experience to be useful to us we then have to fit it in with our previous experience and other knowledge. However, there is no real evidence that we have learnt from any experience until we begin to think about how we might do things differently as a consequence of what we have learned. This final stage, when put into action, leads to a new experience which is another opportunity to learn.

The language used by David Kolb and his colleagues is that of American psychologists so I have chosen the mnemonic **HEMP** instead as a reminder of the way in which we tie together current learning and past experience, in order to manage future events more effectively. What follows is a fuller explanation of the 'Learning From Experience Cycle' and an indication of how it can be used by mentors to enhance the learning of those in their care.

The Experiential Learning Cycle

The four stages anyone, learning from experience, goes through are as follows:

Stage 1 **H**ave an experience.

Stage 2 **E**xamine and reflect upon what has happened.

Stage 3 **M**ake wider sense of the experience by linking it with existing knowledge, previous experience, mental maps, models, theories etc.

Stage 4 Plan how to incorporate the new experience into our repertoire of behaviour or body of knowledge.

1. Have an Experience

Mentors are not normally responsible for the type of experience that a learner receives. The responsible person varies according to the approach being used but it may be

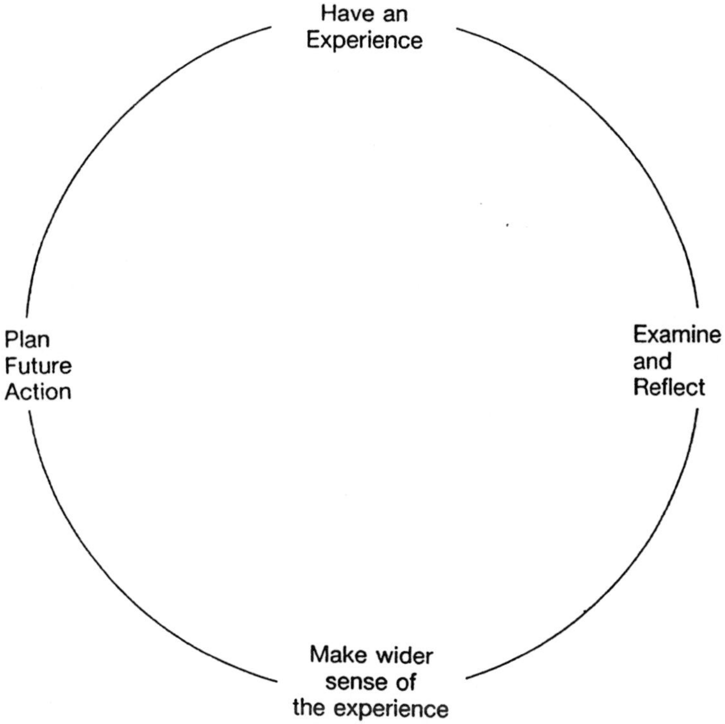

Fig. 3 The Learning From Experience Cycle
(Adapted from Kolb Rubin & McIntyre, Prentice Hall NJ, 1974)

the learner's boss, a training officer or a designated senior manager. Sometimes mentors recognise that their protégé would benefit from taking certain actions or having a particular piece of training or experience, but they must resist the temptation to bring this about. Trying to influence what the learner does will be seen as interference and resented (in most organisations), by the learner's manager or other responsible person. The way to deal with this situation is to help the learner to plan how to get this experience. Doing this not only enhances their self confidence and self-esteem, it teaches them how to get things done within the organisation.

2. Examine and Reflect upon What has Happened

This is, perhaps, the most important stage of the cycle because if someone is unaware of the detail or significance of what has happened, then it is extremely unlikely that they will be able to learn anything from that experience. Mentors help learners to pause, examine in detail and 'take stock' of this particular event or period of time. (This is something a busy boss rarely has enough time to do well.)

It is best to start very generally and be guided by the learner as to what is important for them. Sometimes a mentor will recognise from their own experience that something the learner has done is particularly relevant or important and will seek further information in order to ensure that the appropriate lessons have been learned.

The skilled mentor starts these discussions by making wide use of open-ended questions of the type shown below:

- What have you been doing?

- What have you found particularly interesting since we last met?
- What did you make of that?
- Who else was there/involved?
- What did you see them doing?
- What effect did that have?
- If you had been doing it what would you have done?
- How would people have responded if you had done that? etc.

This example makes it sound a very interrogative process when, of course, in reality it needs to be conversational. This is important because the relationship only works if the learner recognises that they are discussing something of mutual interest with a 'friend'. This experiential learning model and discursive way of relating is the key to the mentor's role. Effective mentors help learners to 'capture' important dimensions of their experience which they can learn from but might otherwise have missed.

3. Make Wider Sense of the Experience

This is the point at which mentors help their learners to pull together their past knowledge and experience, and link it with what is happening currently. It is likely that they also help them to recognise the relevance of what they are learning, to their current or future job and responsibilities.

The mentor's own experience and knowledge becomes most important at this stage of the learning cycle discussion. The mentor's ability to explain procedures, policies, and why certain values are held, is invaluable to a newcomer to the organisation or a particular role. Mentors can help learners to 'see the big picture' and to understand what might otherwise seem arbitrary or irrational.

Managing this stage in a way which enhances their knowledge, without making the learner feel insignificant or inferior, is a vital skill of effective mentors. In essence it means giving information as the learner is ready for it and can use it. It requires that mentors are clear without being pedantic. Most importantly they have to resist the temptation to explain *'how different it all was in their day'*, or in any other way to emphasise the gap there is between them and their learner, in age, experience or knowledge. Mentors must, of course, remain aware of these differences because they effect their relationship with their learner, but alluding to, or commenting upon them, is counter-productive.

4. Plan How to Use New Knowledge, Insights or Skills

In this stage mentors are, primarily, a 'sounding board' to the learner, and they will be using counselling skills and may, if required, move into a coaching role. Experienced mentors know that if the person they are helping is to be committed to any plan of action for making use of experience gained, then it needs to be their own plan. Good mentors help the learner think it through and use their own experience of difficulties and pitfalls, to ensure that the plan anticipates and takes account of problems which may be encountered. Skilled mentors never forget that their learner will learn best from any new experience which follows a plan they have put into action, because they 'own' it completely.

Mentors should guard against the temptation to protect or cosset their learners. It is enough if they ensure, when appropriate, that the learner delays action likely to damage their reputation or career, until after they have helped them

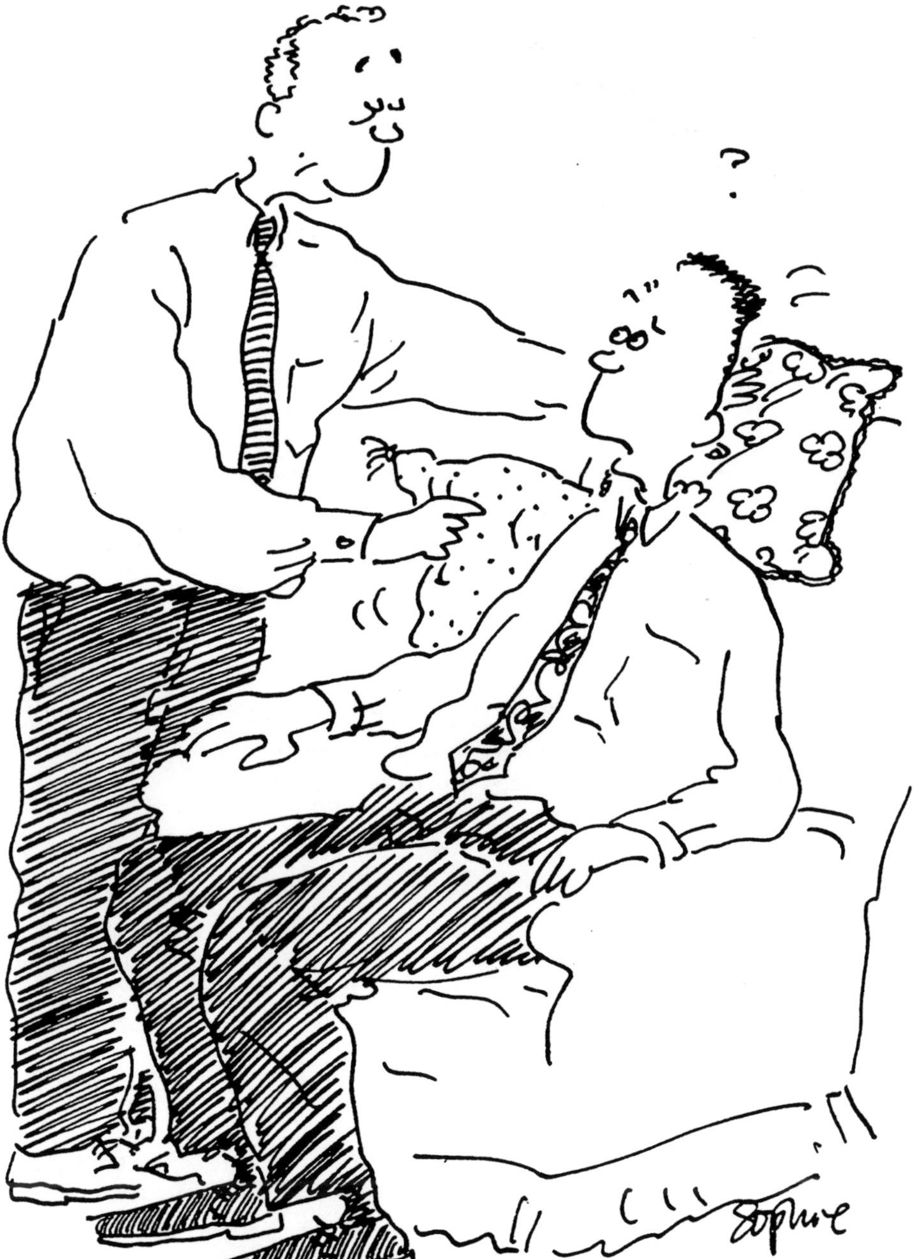

thoroughly explore likely outcomes and their possible consequences.

Finally, mentors need to remember that they are not responsible for what the learner does, their job is to ensure that s/he derives the maximum benefit from the experience, by reviewing it thoroughly using the guidelines given above.

Mentors Need Support

Skilled and competent mentors alone will not ensure the success of a formal mentoring scheme, there does need to be a good support system too. Like many other changes in the way an organisation does things, mentoring works best if it has an influential 'champion'. If this happens to be the most senior manager in the situation, life is comparatively simple because s/he simply uses their executive authority to keep the initiative moving. Careful communication with potential mentors, learners and those who supervise them is still vital. This needs to cover:

- Why it is being done (the need being addressed);
- What it is designed to achieve (objectives);
- Who is to be involved and why (This may include specification or profile of both mentors and potential learners – what qualifies them to do the job/be involved);
- The specific responsibility of each of the parties involved;
- The 'ground rules' on confidentiality and other issues which will apply, etc.

Where the 'champion' of a mentoring scheme does not have executive authority the situation is more difficult. An enthusiastic young human relations specialist recently saw months of work, investigating how mentoring schemes worked in similar 'high-tech' companies, come to nought because no section of the company was prepared to run a 'pilot' scheme as s/he recommended.

The problem in this company was, apart from the pace of rapid change which seemed to be part of their way of life, that no **specific** need had been identified. The study was set up because senior managers had a genuine desire to be sure that they were doing things as well as they could but, unlike the BP Chemicals example cited earlier, there was no concrete evidence that there were problems or issues which could be solved by mentoring.

This is the first essential. Few organisations in the modern world are able to avoid technological, economic and legislative change, so they are reluctant to embark on any scheme (yet another change), which offers vague promises of benefits derived by other organisations. First gather your evidence of the need within your own organisation, and then tie the desired benefits firmly to this evidence, seems to be the first lesson.

Once the idea has been accepted there are still potential pitfalls. Administrative details like who facilitates the first meeting between mentor and learner, are particularly important with company newcomers. One organisation discovered that more than four months had elapsed before this first meeting occurred. If the learner had experienced any 'entry' problems s/he would either have solved them alone or left the company. This case had a happy outcome because a relationship was established which proved very helpful when the learner's first job change occurred several months later. When asked about the early experience the learner said, *'I thought that mention of mentoring was simply a recruitment gimmick'*, and the mentor's view was that the learner *'must be OK as s/he had not been in touch'*. As mentioned earlier British Airways ensured that mentors and learners met during the latter's initial training period. One BP Chemicals site organised a informal lunch for all mentors and learners as a means of introducing them to each other. Another company which offered mentoring to new employees, made it clear that it was the boss's responsibility to take the newcomer to the mentor's place of work and effect an introduction. It was stressed that this should happen during the new employee's first week.

There are a variety of ways in which these important details can be handled and experience shows that if they are overlooked, the mentoring scheme will founder. Managers have too many other things on their minds. The early stages of (formal) mentoring are fraught with difficulty for both mentors and learners because it is not a 'natural' relationship. It only becomes mutually satisfying once it is established. For this reason alone a number of organisations are very specific about the frequency and timing of the first six or so meetings.

Summary

Mentors, in effect, focus on and expand a small part of the manager's job. They do this by giving time and a quality of attention to their learner which few managers could afford the time to do. They can do this at a level of mutual trust, which no manager with responsibility for getting results is likely to achieve. It is important to remember when introducing a formal mentoring scheme that most will fail if they do not have substantial support from senior managers, as well as the cooperation of those who supervise those being mentored.

The Learning Cycle above is a good model for all discussions between mentor and learner; it provides a structure for most agendas they are likely to have. Chapter 3 gives specific guidelines and advice on how the first meeting should be conducted. It focuses more strongly on the way in which good mentors relate to those they are helping and stresses the need to listen carefully, suspend judgement and allow the learner to do most of the talking.

3 Getting Started

Introduction

Getting started on mentoring is difficult. This will not surprise many people, because most of us know that any change is difficult for both individuals and organisations. Mentoring is a change for mentors, their learners and those who manage them. Some of what has been written on coping with change underpins this chapter, but it concentrates specifically upon the difficulties which can occur, when trying to make a start on developing people in this way.

It goes on to describe some of the steps which different British companies and public bodies have taken, to make sure that their formal mentoring schemes did not founder on the rocks of line management opposition, indifference, or poor administration. Finally, it suggests a set of steps to follow which can help mentors get their relationship with the person they are to help, off to a good start.

Chapters 1 and 2 have alluded to opposition by managers to formal mentoring schemes which stems from the feeling that mentors are intruding upon the manager's role. This is not simply intransigence on the part of people opposing a new approach to staff development. Many employers these days seem to be trying to do more with less staff, as they exploit new technology and battle to remain competitive. Often this results in increased pressure on those employees who are left and mentoring is yet another demand on the time of those involved, even if there are overall time savings and other benefits to be gained.

Managers, mentors and learners can all have reservations and concerns about mentoring. Some of these of these are listed below.

Managers of Learners

Will the confidential relationship between learner and mentor result in:

- Me missing out on information which would help to develop and manage this staff member more effectively?
- The learner discussing my performance with the mentor? (often one of the manager's peers).
- Split loyalty on the part of this employee?

Is the fact that they require a mentor a criticism of my performance?

How will I keep control with learners away from work at odd times?

Mentors

- Will I have the time to do this well?
- Will it cause me to be isolated from my peers?
- Do I have the skills required?
- Will I be embarrassed and have difficulty coping if my learner experiences personal or emotional problems?
- Will the organisation give me and this initiative sufficient support?
- I know it is a confidential relationship, but what do I do if . . . (a wide range of concerns like 'my learner (a valued employee) tells me they want to leave', etc.
- What if I don't like my learner?

Learners

- Is having a mentor a sign of weakness?
- Does this mean that they don't really trust me as a responsible person?
- Can I trust my mentor?
- How much is it safe to reveal?
- Will what I say get back to my boss or in some other way damage my prospects?
- Do I have the time, or will it undermine my work effort?
- How will my boss react – is s/he really in favour of this?

The First Meeting

Experienced mentors know that their first meeting with the person they are to help is vital in getting the 'friendship' off to a good start. In 'normal' social situations people either strike a spark and establish rapport, or they do not pursue the relationship. Informal mentoring only occurs where there is mutual respect and regard, but formal mentoring schemes, initially at least, flout convention and ask those involved to 'manufacture' a friendship.

To begin with, the relationship between mentor and learner is very uneven, particularly if the learner is new to the company; care must still be taken with experienced or more senior employees, but they are less likely to be daunted by status differences or 'trappings of office' The mentor has most of the information and virtually all of the power, as far as the success of this first meeting is concerned. Competent mentors therefore pay particular attention to the relationship building skills of showing respect, expressing understanding, and being genuine.

They try ensure that the environment, seating arrangements and the quality of the attention they give their learners will result in them feeling relaxed quickly. They want to show learners that their interest in them is genuine.

Readers new to mentoring may find the mnemonic **WASP** a useful guide to help them plan and conduct this first interview:

Welcome Setting the person at ease.

Acquire Finding out about the other person; their background, experience, hopes/fears and expectations.

Supply Telling the other person as much as necessary about yourself, for them to feel that you have had a worthwhile conversation.

Part Winding up the meeting in a way which makes the other person feel that their time has been well spent and that yours has not been wasted.

Most importantly, that you and s/he have a clear understanding of what will happen when, where and why you next meet.

Welcome

The mentor sets the person they are to help at ease by ensuring that there is ample time, free from interruption. In some situations mentors have found it more sensible to meet the learner away from their office/work station. The practice in British Airways varied enormously according to the job the mentor had and the location of the trainee at any particular time.

Those mentors who have a suitable office do not, if possible, stay behind their desk because they know that it can create a barrier and emphasise any status difference there is between them and the learner. If for some reason (lack of space) they have to meet their learner at their desk, they ensure that the minimum desk space (perhaps only the corner) separates them.

The first meeting works best when mentors make their opening questions very general and entirely social; e.g. 'How are you getting on?' 'Where are you living?' etc. Experienced mentors also seek to establish some link with the learner which might speed up the process of establishing rapport. It can be sporting, educational, geographical or any other point of contact or shared experience; any topic which allows the learner to speak as an equal because they know as much about that subject as the mentor. Practice varies, but at Albright & Wilson all mentors had met their learners during the recruitment process and therefore had the basis already for a relationship. Another company encourages mentors to study the application form and other data on their learner as part of their preparation for this meeting. A third which recruits graduates for careers rather than jobs, had interviewers indicate on the interview report forms whether they would be prepared to mentor this candidate if they were hired, in addition to whether they would be prepared to have them start their career in her/his department).

Good mentors are careful to use any prior information they have discreetly and not to carry out an interrogation. They stay with a particular subject for some time and respond in a genuine way to any information they obtain. For example, if they know the learner's school, university, members of staff, their previous employer, home town etc; they say so briefly, and turn the conversation back to the learner.

They also sit in a relaxed manner, maintain regular eye contact and are careful not take notes in the presence of the learner, because this can cause a break-down in rapport. Finally, they move on to specific, work related topics, only once they see that the person they are helping has relaxed.

Acquire

It is important that mentors get to know as much as possible about their learners. If they are young and new to the organisation it may be perfectly appropriate to learn about their family background, school, university, vacation or other work experience. In other mentoring situations this may not be necessary, but the key is to share information which will help the rapid development of the relationship. The word *share* is important, because the learner has to be treated with the respect that would be shown to any new acquaintance. It is not acceptable, in our society, to simply 'pump someone for information' without in some way matching the degree of openness and trust that is being asked of them.

A helpful and 'safe' topic for the first meeting with a learner is to find out what they know about the formal mentoring system of which you are both part and to dispel any myths they have about how it works. Sometimes with new recruits there will be anxieties about it being part of some plot to weed out people who should not have been selected. There may be a belief that the mentor is going to report on their progress and if this is the case it destroys totally the mentor's capacity to be really helpful.

In addition to the Mentoring Scheme, it is useful to find out what the learner knows about the work-place, your department and the organisation in general. In fact, anything at all which might give you insight into what kind of person they are, and how they are feeling right at this moment. Another advantage of these topics is that they are all likely to lead to genuine two-way conversations, which leave the learner feeling that it was worthwhile talking with the mentor.

Supply

New mentors need to be wary that, because learners want to know so much, and mentors realise how much they have to tell them, this third stage could take up a major proportion of the time they spend together. It is the responsibility of mentors to ensure that this does not happen. In most mentoring schemes the relationship is going to last a comparatively long time, and there will be ample opportunity for the learner to hear about their mentor's career, circumstances, hopes and ambitions. It surprises some people new to the mentor role that these are legitimate subjects for discussion, but one advantage the mentor has over the boss is that they can be more open including, if appropriate, showing some human frailty without losing any credibility.

Experienced mentors do respond to genuine interest/ questions from those they are helping, but otherwise they restrict themselves to brief relevant references to anything their learner says. They recognise that the only really important information they have to give at this meeting is about Mentoring; their understanding of it, and how they plan to make it work for their learner.

Part

Experienced mentors have discovered that the single most important aspect of this final stage, is arranging the next meeting for a specific time and place. Mentors can find their diaries filling up for weeks ahead and new mentoring relationships are too fragile to cope with postponed, hastily convened or rushed meetings. Secondly, mentors report on the value of being clear about not only what their expectations of the learner will be at this next meeting, but also what they can expect of the mentor. The mentor–learner relationship faces more hazards at this stage of its life than *Sonic the Hedgehog* and therefore requires very careful nurturing by mentors.

Finally, as soon as the learner has left, good mentors make any brief notes necessary to ensure that they will remember important personal details, and will be able to plan for an effective second meeting. One learner complained, *'It was as if each meeting dropped into a black hole – s/he never ever referred to a previous meeting or enquired about how I had got on with something we'd discussed'*.

Summary

Mentors at their first meeting with learners spend most of their time finding out about the other person in a neutral, low/key and unthreatening manner. (They spend, at most, 25% of the total time together supplying information.) They try to ensure that those being mentored come away from this first meeting feeling that the mentor has their best interests at heart; s/he is someone they can both relate to and trust; a potential friend.

So far I have dealt only with the values and style of mentoring and provided guidance for the first meeting. It is not possible to be prescriptive about any other meeting because the content of the second and subsequent meetings will, in the main, be determined by the person being mentored and what has happened since learner and mentor last met. For this reason mentors always need to have a flexible plan and re-reading the summary to Chapter 2 and the information on 'The Experiential Learning Cycle' from time to time, may prove helpful.

However, the form and style of all meetings are firmly in the hands of the mentor and the remaining chapters will provide help with ensuring that these go well.

4

Helping Learners Make Good Use of Resources

Introduction

If you are new to mentoring you may feel, from what has been written so far, that the mentor–learner relationship sounds very personal, perhaps even precious and have doubts about your willingness to participate or your suitability for the role. This is not an uncommon reaction, many mentors being introduced to a formal mentoring programme feel this way.

This chapter will provide a broader perspective on the relationship. It examines specifically the way in which networking can maximise a learner's ability to benefit from their experience. It warns against introducing networking skills too soon and suggests that this technique can ensure that the learner does not become too dependent upon their mentor, or the relationship become too intense. Finally, it provides a list of questions which may be found useful by those who are new to mentoring, or who do not think of themselves as effective 'networkers'.

Defining the Relationship

Defining the desired nature of the mentor–learner relationship in formal mentoring schemes has proved difficult for some organisations, leading to early confusion on the part of mentors and others involved. One company laid such heavy stress on confidentiality at the start of their programme, that mentors believed that they were not allowed to talk to each other.

Obviously no mentor would discuss personal details of their learner with another, but these mentors would have been much more effective helpers if they had been able to swap notes on some of their early successes and difficulties. One company made a point of arranging regular meetings of mentors with the scheme's champion, who was a resource in case of difficulty.

At these meetings mentors revealed some of their doubts or successes and were able to benefit from each other's experience. For example, one person mentioned that s/he felt that there was still considerable reserve on the part of their learner and another had simply resolved this same problem by taking the learner for a drink after work. The person responsible for the scheme was able at these meetings to give guidance on issues like this and clarify policy.

In another company the value of these review meetings was quickly proven. Soon after the scheme started some of the mentors were sent appraisal forms to complete for their learners. One mentor was quite clear; he sent the form back to its sender explaining that assessment was the job of the boss alone. Two mentors were uncertain and one was of the opinion that he should complete the assessment because *'I know him better than his boss does'*. The discussion which followed was very lively but it finished with agreement, consistency and a group of mentors who, although they were new to the role, understood the nature of their relationship with their learner very well indeed.

I like to think that all experienced mentors would recognise that in not talking to others with similar responsibilities, they were behaving very uncharacteristically. One of the key skills that any mentor can teach a learner is to make good use of the resources available to them and to be wide ranging in identifying people who have knowledge, skills or other information which could improve the results they achieve.

Young people in particular, sometimes have concerns about the idea of exploiting friends, colleagues and acquaintances and it would seem distasteful and manipulative to many of us to cultivate people, simply because of what they could do for us. On the other hand, most of us have certain people in our lives whom we would always seek out on particular issues. We may have discussions with, or seek advice and practical help from, those we respect and whom we know to have relevant experience or resources. This seems like common sense and because we are clear about our motives, and sincere in our respect for the other person, not at all exploitative.

One young graduate in the BP Chemicals scheme was quite clear about the benefits. She said, *'My mentor has many years experience in the company and knows a good many people, as well as being skilled in knowing how to go about getting things done'*. A mentor in the same company reflected that she made extensive use of her network in order to help her learner and said, *'I find that from time to time it is more useful to direct my learner towards someone else in the organisation rather than seek the information myself'*.

When mentors work in this way they ensure that learners do not become dependent upon them and they help the learners begin to build a network which may be useful and last far longer than the formal mentoring relationship.

What is Networking?

The term 'Networking' has become an increasingly popular phrase since the eighties, but it is a new name for a very old idea which featured in 'Self-Improvement' books written by people like Dale Carnegie in the 1930s. This long history does not in any way diminish its usefulness because it is a simple, commonsense strategy for making the greatest possible use of the resources available.

The recent emphasis on networking is based, in part, on management research. This indicated that very effective general managers always work on a wide-ranging agenda of things that they want to get done, and that they identify, monitor and accomplish these tasks through an informal network of contacts at all levels throughout the organisation. This whole process relies heavily on contacts which have been built up throughout the manager's career as he has moved around and up the organisation.

The subjects in these studies were male, and the difference between their career paths and those of females in the same organisations, helped to increase awareness of the importance and relevance of 'networking' in the modern world. Organisations trying to advance the careers of females and other minority groups, realised the significance of this difference in work experience; their careers had been much less mobile both geographically and functionally and they had not therefore developed an extensive network 'naturally'. Members of these groups were encouraged to take the initiative in seeking out those who could help their careers. They were also encouraged to collaborate as well as compete with one another; to use each other as a resource. In other words to start work on developing their network.

The rapid growth of self-employment and small businesses following the 1980s recession in the UK was another influence. Entrepreneurs were encouraged by government agencies and training organisations to form self-help groups, and to spend time reflecting upon their past careers and present acquaintances, in order to identify those who might prove of help; those contacts who might make the difference between success and failure. Lastly, the unemployed have been encouraged to join 'Job Clubs'. In these cases there has been as much emphasis on giving, as receiving help, but most advice to people on networking, regrettably, lacks this emphasis.

Many of us have extensive networks of our own, and form part of someone else's without even thinking about it much. Most of us are helpers as well as helped. Even when the advice and assistance seems to be flowing in one direction only, there are often benefits for the person giving help. Sometimes it is new clarity on a subject, or insight into a different part of the organisation. One mentor reported that s/he realised that the advice s/he was giving had a wider and more personal application. Other mentors surveyed have reported these and other benefits which have come from their role as part of a learner's developing network.

Mentors are in a prime position to ensure that someone new to the organisation or to a specific job does not feel that s/he is being either weak or manipulative, when s/he seeks help or makes use of other people's skills and experience. Skilled mentors help learners to identify the benefits of working with and through others, and also to develop the skills necessary to do this effectively. They are able, with their knowledge of the organisation and extensive contacts, to get the learner's 'network' off to a good start. Finally, mentors can help young employees to understand what the term 'networking' means within their organisation, and encourage them to value teamwork as well as individual effort.

How is Networking Done?

If you are new to mentoring, or have not thought a good deal about the way in which you have developed and use your own network, you may find it helpful to reflect for a moment upon the old definition of management as 'getting things done, with and through others'. It seems to me that this definition increasingly applies to employees at all levels in most modern organisations. No one has the monopoly on creativity and problem-solving ability. Very few people have jobs which are not reliant in some way on receiving help and cooperation from others.

The term 'internal customer' is used by many organisations to emphasise this inter-dependence, which must work fruitfully, if high quality results are to be achieved. Mentors to young, new employees recognise that their experience ot cooperation is unlikely to have extended much beyond lending notes to a friend who has missed a lecture, or collaboration on a project with a small team which may have been in competition with other teams.

The mentor has to help these young people recognise the value of cooperation with others and smooth their transition from 'star' to 'team-player'. Experienced mentors keep this in mind whenever they are discussing issues with their learner. They continually ask themselves a number of key questions and as time progresses encourage learners to ask these questions of themselves. Some of these are:

- Who do I know who knows about this?
- Who do I know who has experience – has done this, or something similar?
- Who is likely to be affected by the proposed action?
  - How will they be affected – positively – negatively?
  - What power do they have to help or hinder?
  - What is the source and nature of their power, and

how can this be harnessed – focused – neutralized – circumvented?

- Who do I know who has access to relevant resources?
- Who do I know who knows someone who has experience?
- What have I done personally that might be relevant or useful?

Readers will note that their own knowledge and experience comes last. This is because experienced mentors know that it will frequently be more developmental for the learner to extend their personal network. They can learn lessons which will serve them in the long term if they use someone else as a resource, rather than take the easy option of tapping into the expertise of their mentor.

Mentors find that it is usually wise not to begin this 'network development' until after they have established a relationship of mutual trust and confidence with their learner. Done too soon, it could undermine the relationship and the mentor's credibility, because learners who are referred to others too often and too soon, could feel that their mentor was not really interested in them.

Experienced mentors also recognise that there is a degree of risk in allowing someone they do not know well to have direct access to their network. They wait until they have begun to trust the learner's judgement and ask themselves questions like:

- How should the person to whom I am referring my learner, be approached in order to ensure a successful outcome?

- Do I need to check how my learner plans to do this?
- Are there any pitfalls of which I need to make her/him aware?
- How is the person to whom I am referring likely to view the approach?

- How will this affect the way in which my 'contact' perceives or relates to me?
- Do I need to speak with the person to whom I am referring my learner, or do anything (before or after the event), in order to protect or enhance my relationship with that person?
- How will it affect my learner's credibility, or their relationship, if I speak directly with my 'contact' – even if it is simply to acknowledge their support/ cooperation?
- A final question may be: 'What is the added value of this referral likely to be – to the learner; to the person referred to; to me (the mentor) or to the organisation?'

Summary

Surveys show that the formal mentoring schemes which work best are those which incorporate regular reviews, so that mentors are able to 'network' and learn from each other's experience. It is not easy to decide which of the skills used by mentors is most important but, in terms of reward for effort alone, 'networking' must rate very highly indeed. It is clear that a key task for mentors is helping someone who is new to a job or organisation establish an effective network, because this not only makes learners effective more quickly, but also ensures that they do not become too dependent on their mentors. To be truly effective in doing this they have to be sure that they are helping their learner to realise her/his full potential; it is not enough to simply 'open doors for them'.

Cooperating and collaborating does not always come naturally to those who are new to the world of work. Actions that an experienced person may take for granted, may not be thought of by a young or inexperienced learner. Even when a learner recognises the need to work through others, s/he may not know how to do this well. They may need help in developing this ability. Providing this assistance can involve mentors in the important skill of coaching, which is dealt with in the next chapter.

5

Mentor as Coach

Introduction

Many people new to mentoring feel more comfortable about the mentor's role as coach, than most other aspects of the job. This may be because it is clear and familiar to those with management experience in particular. They see it as a central activity in meeting their mentor responsibilities and are confident about their ability. However, it is in many ways, the most difficult task of all for mentors.

Its familiarity is one source of difficulty, because even experienced mentors are tempted to 'teach' when counselling would be more appropriate. It is also difficult for mentors to remain clear about their legitimate domain and that of the line manager; the learner's boss.

This chapter will provide greater clarity on this dilemma by defining coaching and providing guidelines for being effective, when using it to help others to grow and develop. It identifies why it is a difficult issue and offers advice on how to be an effective coach, without interfering in line management areas of responsibility.

What is Coaching?

Coaching is a way of improving someone's performance by identifying and tackling **skill** deficiencies. The word 'skill' is emphasised here because although coaching techniques can be used when trying to fill gaps in knowledge, it is most effective when the person being helped has to *do* something. We all know that 'practice makes perfect' but this pre-supposes that what is being practised is correct. Coaching is an active, initiative-taking, set of skills best summed up by one athlete, who said that her coach experienced everything except the pain. Coaches accept some responsibility for the development of their pupils and therefore require relevant knowledge and experience.

Purists would say that it is the only way to help another improve their skill. My own view is that counsellors without any 'job-related' skills can, in certain circumstances, help people to understand what they are doing wrong and identify what they need to do instead – but that is the subject of the next chapter.

Ideally a coach should see someone perform before attempting to help them improve. However, some world class athletes live in different countries from their coaches and mentors rarely have the opportunity to see the person they are helping 'in action'. As a mentor, you are most likely to coach in anticipation of an event, about which the other person has expressed some anxiety. A BP Chemicals mentor provided a typical example when he said, *'I have been able to help my learner prepare for an important meeting and steer him round some of the pitfalls he might otherwise have encountered'*.

It will be useful to start by examining a 'pure' model of the coaching process, so that it easier to understand just what mentors have to do in order to coach effectively.

The Four Stages of Coaching

1. **Observation** – the coach sees, in detail, the level of performance and area for improvement.

2. **Analysis** – the cause of poor performance is identified and understood.

3. **Modelling** – the coach demonstrates or explains correct performance.

4. **Practice and Review** – the new behaviour is tried out under supervision.

Observation

Even if a coach is unable to see the person they are helping in action, there are certain things s/he must know in order to be effective. Firstly, they need to know in detail, what action the person took. Secondly, they need to know precisely what results were obtained. Lastly, they have to understand comprehensively the conditions in which these results were obtained.

Analysis

This stage is important, because if people are to improve their performance, they must understand not only what they are doing wrong, but also what they are not doing right. This is the key skill of the coach. Is your experience like mine, that the world at large seems to have no difficulty in telling you when you have done something wrong? Some may be able to specify **precisely** your incorrect actions or inappropriate behaviour, but skilled coaches can tell you what you should do in order to improve.

Modelling

Great boxing champions like Henry Cooper and Muhammad Ali were coached to success by men who would have been receiving a pension in any other walk of life. These small, elderly men could not physically demonstrate what was required, so modelling is clearly more than 'just watch me and you'll soon pick it up'. What these people were able to do was describe **precisely** what had to be done, demonstrate (in slow motion) and observe acutely when the move was practiced.

Practice and Review

The greatest improvement occurs when the new behaviour takes place as soon as possible after it has been learned. Learning is accelerated when the coach is present and is able to provide encouragement and correction. If this feedback and advice can only be given during a role play, rehearsal or other practice, then mentors have to rely upon hearing of plans before, and results after, the actual event.

How is Coaching Done?

To re-phrase what was said before, coaches help others to identify ways in which they are underperforming, recognise what has to be done differently and practice the skills and actions necessary to achieve this improvement. Coaches need to know the task or skills involved, be able to identify and specify what someone is doing wrong, and state clearly the steps they need to take in order to improve.

If the coach is to be successful, then the way in which this is done is equally important and requires additional skills. They have to be able to give feed-back in a way which is understandable, actionable and motivating. A learner who does not understand what they are being told, does not see how (or believe) they can do what is required, or feels disparaged or discouraged, will not progress. Coaches have to be able to relate to those they are helping, so that they can understand how they are feeling, and give them the support required to help them through particular learning or other difficulties.

To sum up, as a coach you want to create a situation in which someone can, without any loss of self-esteem acknowledge a deficiency, recognise how they need to change, and feel that this change is both possible and desirable.

In order to accomplish this, effective coaches go through four stages. They are:

- **Set the person at ease**
- **Specify the performance gap**
- **Provide the opportunity to practice**
- **Evaluate performance and give feedback**

Those new to coaching will find it helpful to look at each of these stages in more detail and experienced managers who are mentoring for the first time, may find it useful to examine their current coaching practice in the light of what follows.

Stage 1 – Set the Person at Ease

Coaches do this by:

- giving the person concerned their undivided attention in a private setting;
- listening to their account of the difficulty they are experiencing and trying to understand how they feel about it;
- acknowledging their feelings and putting their difficulty into context (preferably by citing difficulties the coach has experienced personally).

The aim is to separate the person from the problem so that they can feel 'OK' about themselves even if they feel 'not OK' about the performance area.

Stage 2 – Specify the Performance Gap

Wise coaches involve their 'pupil' as much as they can rather than simply tell them what is wrong. They do this, in part, in order to ensure their commitment; it can indicate that the learner accepts the need to improve. It also helps develop, in the learner, this self-critical, analytical skill. The steps for this stage are:

- Get the 'pupil' to describe in detail the action (behaviour) they are taking (using), the results they are achieving and any circumstances likely to influence these results.

- Help them to identify the action (behaviour) which they intend to take (use) and specify how this will result in the desired outcome(s).

- If necessary, take them back through the circumstances they described in order to check that their proposed action seems sensible and likely to have the desired effect.

Stage 3 – Provide Opportunity to Practice

Experienced coaches try to make this an opportunity to learn from success. 'Trial and error' may roll off the tongue nicely and have a familiar ring, but 'trial and success' is a much more effective way to learn.

So good coaches:

- ensure that practice takes place as soon as possible after the coaching session;
- try to provide a low-risk environment, which may involve role-playing a situation with the person they are helping, or perhaps, setting up a 'dry-run' where failure does not matter;
- if they cannot be present when practice occurs, they help the person identify some performance indicators, i.e. 'milestones', which will confirm to the learner that they are on course for success.

As a mentor you will almost never have the opportunity to see your learner putting a coached skill into action, but Stage 4 below is equally valid for a 'rehearsal' or any other practice you provide.

Stage 4 – Evaluate Performance and Give Feedback

Giving feedback is a highly skilled process which requires you to describe the behaviour you have seen, help the person you are coaching to understand the consequences of this behaviour and gain their agreement to the action necessary to remedy the situation. Again it is useful to look at each one of these steps in detail.

Describe the Behaviour

The coach describes what s/he saw, as specifically as possible, and in as much detail as necessary, so that the person receiving the feedback can understand the difference between what they are doing, and what they should be doing.

Effective coaches get the learner to start this process and do as much as possible themselves, even if the coach has been present and seen what has occurred. As mentioned earlier, this tells the coach how much they understand and what further information or help still has to be provided. It also ensures that the person being coached has as much 'ownership' as possible of what still has to be done.

Specify the Consequences

Coaches say, in effect, 'Because you did . . . . . this . . . . . occurred'. Again it is wiser to have the person being coached specify the consequences of their actions by asking, 'What effect did that have?', or a similar question.

NB: This is an important stage, because some inexperienced people will know that they are not doing something quite correctly, but may feel that it does not matter. It may be that some possible consequences have not occurred this time and that they need help in understanding what could happen.

Agree What Needs to be Done

Experienced coaches know that specificity is important here and they will always try to get their 'pupil' to describe in detail what they plan to do in order to improve. The person being coached needs to understand, completely, what has to be done. General statements like 'I will listen more carefully' or 'You need to improve your ability to listen' are no good. It may have to be: 'I will establish eye contact with the speaker, show that I am listening, by nodding and murmuring appropriately, etc, and if the person speaking seems to feel strongly about what they are saying, or I disagree with their views, I will acknowledge their feelings and paraphrase what they have said before I reply.'

All of the above assumes that the mentor is dealing with someone who is aware that things are not as they should be, and wants to do something about the situation. This is usually the case, but life is not always so simple. On occasion we have to start by making someone aware that their performance is below par. Managers often find themselves having to convince another person that there is a gap between their performance and the desired standard. They may be faced with someone who cannot see a need to change. Mentors are more likely to find themselves in the situation described by one learner: *'I asked for help from my mentor – she gave me really good advice and helped by encouraging me to practice and rehearse something I had been quite apprehensive about – it worked out really well in the end.'*

If the need does arise to give unsolicited feedback or coaching, the procedure to follow is more complex, because the feedback may be experienced by the learner as an attack on their self-esteem, or it may not be believed. Whenever mentors feel the need to **initiate** feedback or coaching they must first ask themselves 'Is this my business?'. Their second question must be 'Is this the right time?'

A useful starting point for answering the first question is the rule of thumb that all 'technical or specific subject' difficulties are the boss's province and difficulties in the social skill area (those related to people – including the learner themselves, their self-awareness and honesty), are likely to be an appropriate coaching subject for the mentor. If asked for help with technical, work-related problems, experienced mentors help the learner find ways of harnessing the boss's coaching skills.

To answer the second question, mentors have to decide which is at greater risk – the learner's career if the issue is not tackled, or the mentoring relationship if it is?

Tackling Performance Problems

It is probably worth re-stating that mentors have no direct responsibility for how a learner performs. Job performance and development of job-related skills are the responsibility of the line manager. However, it is perfectly legitimate to tackle a learner about how they are meeting their responsibilities within the mentoring relationship; e.g. persistently arriving late for, or failing to attend meetings. Some mentors report that the person they are trying to help is consistently unrealistic in assessing their progress; they claim achievements or knowledge which is not borne out by the evidence available. One described 'the kick in the pants'

given to a learner whose career was in jeopardy, *'because he did not understand the seriousness of his situation and was deluding himself about his boss's feedback on his performance'*.

When mentors tackle these issues it is a rare excursion out of their role of 'non-judgemental friend' and is unlikely to be appropriate in the early months of the relationship. The steps necessary to do this effectively are very similar to those above but there is a difference in the style used by mentors who have to supplement their careful attention and active listening with assertive, fact **giving** behaviour. This means that mentors have to:

Stage 1 – Describe Behaviour and Results

- Be specific about what they are doing and the effect this is having.
- Own the feed-back by using 'I' (feel, disapprove, etc), not quote company policy or make general statements about what others expect, do, etc.
- Listen to and acknowledge the learner's explanation of influencing factors, or other excuses; this is best done by reiterating or paraphrasing what they have said.
  - e.g. 'You are saying . . . . .' or 'You feel . . . . .'. The mentor then expresses her/his own view including, if appropriate, repeating the feed-back.
- Have the learner summarise what has been said and suggest a possible solution.
- Boost their self-esteem by identifying relevant aspects of performance which are going well, the merit of their proposed solution, or perhaps by acknowledging the difficulty of what they are tackling.

Stage 2 – Seek Agreement on Performance Gap

- Get them to acknowledge (and provide evidence to support their acceptance of the fact), that the feedback is accurate.
- Have them restate and agree the expected standard. If they do not know it or cannot specify it, tell them what is required and get them to agree that it is reasonable and/or desirable.
- Tell them of the reasons for requiring the specific standard to be met and outline the consequences of non-compliance, if they have difficulty in accepting it.

- Compliment them upon their performance on some past occasion in a related area, or make a more general statement of genuine appreciation of them as a person.

Stage 3 – Agree a Plan of Action

- Discuss and agree specific action steps.
- Decide upon some performance indicators which will help them to know that they are 'on track', and enable you to assess their future performance.
- Decide upon a review date and agree the form this review will take.
- Encourage their efforts by complimenting them upon the clarity of their plan, or in some other appropriate way which emphasises that they are appreciated as individuals, despite the earlier disapproval of their behaviour; i.e. keep the person separate from the problem.

Experienced mentors know that it is important throughout this entire process to remember what was said originally about maintaining the self-esteem of the person they are helping. Setting them at ease, helping them to put the 'coached' skill into action, assessing performance and providing helpful feedback are just as relevant to the person who is unaware of their deficiencies as they are to the 'willing improver'.

Summary

It is important that mentors remember always that they are not responsible for their learner's work performance. Most of the coaching they do is as a helpful friend. It is equally important to remember that, regardless of the situation, coaching works best when the coach is supportive throughout and encourages the other person by making them feel they 'can do it'. On the rare occasions when mentors do provide feedback and coaching which has not been sought, they need to be sure that they are not intruding upon the line manager's domain, or permanently damaging their relationship with their protégé.

6

Mentor as Counsellor

Introduction

The skills of the counsellor lie at the heart of the mentor's role. These skills are the key to the mentor being able to help their learners cope with early difficulties, make the best possible use of the learning opportunities and build a solid foundation for their future growth during the period of the mentoring relationship. Using the techniques of the counsellor, they empower their learners by reducing their uncertainty, building their confidence and liberating them from inappropriate anxiety caused by low self-esteem or unclear goals.

Unfortunately counselling is an over-used and misunderstood term. People and organisations selling goods and services use it to seem more professional. Some people use it to mean giving advice or sharing their experience. *'What I would do if I were you . . .'* One company never dismisses anyone but it does occasionally 'counsel people out of the organisation'. For others, counselling is done by 'agony aunts' or 'do-gooders', when people have personal, emotional problems. My own view is that it is a very tough-minded and practical form of help, which can be useful in a variety of situations, but can only be given by one mature person to another.

This chapter will expand upon this view of counselling. It will stress that the vocabulary and skills of the counsellor are those that you could hear on the top of the 'Clapham Omnibus'. Only the context in which the mentor uses them is different. No amount of reading can turn an untrained person into a counsellor. That would take *at least* a one-year full-time course. However, what follows will provide guidance to mentors on how to use the skills of the counsellor. It also discusses the relationship and overlap between coaching and counselling.

What is Counselling?

Counselling is a way of helping people to help themselves. Its four main aims are to help someone:

- see their present situation more clearly;
- understand fully how they feel about it;
- determine what, if anything, they want to do about it;
- and make realistic plans for achieving what they want.

When counselling skills are used to help someone think

something through, there is an underlying assumption that they have the skills, knowledge and desire to solve the problem, but that these abilities and qualities are impeded for some reason. The impediment may be no more than the **belief** that they do not know, or cannot do, what is required. They may be too close to the problem, or too immersed in the emotion attached to it, to be able to use their intellect and rational thinking abilities to the full.

The essence of the counselling relationship is that the attention given to the other person enables them to 'step back' from the problem or issue and work their way through these 'blocks' until they can see clearly what they should do.

Mentors report having helped individuals think through a wide range of life events and difficulties. These include relating more effectively to colleagues and boss, career choices, house purchase and other accommodation options, and significant changes in their social life. In all of these situations mentors have been able to provide a neutral ear.

Mentors also use the skills of the counsellor during their regular meetings with learners. These techniques are the ideal way to ensure that the fullest possible discussion takes place at each stage of the learning cycle described in Chapter 2. This enhances learning because the result is a very thorough exploration of the learner's experience.

Most importantly, when someone is counselled it is **their** brain that does the analysis, and draws the conclusions. Although the mentor may help the learner to take a broader perspective or identify some workable solution, the learner gains in confidence, because whatever they decide to do is a product of their own intellect and effort.

This is the major difference between counselling and coaching; the skills used by coach and counsellor overlap, but the underlying assumptions are quite different and as a consequence, each uses techniques and skills which the other does not.

The simplified model (Figure 4) illustrates the primary difference between these ways of helping and shows the skill overlap which exists, because of the styles a mentor may adopt when using either technique.

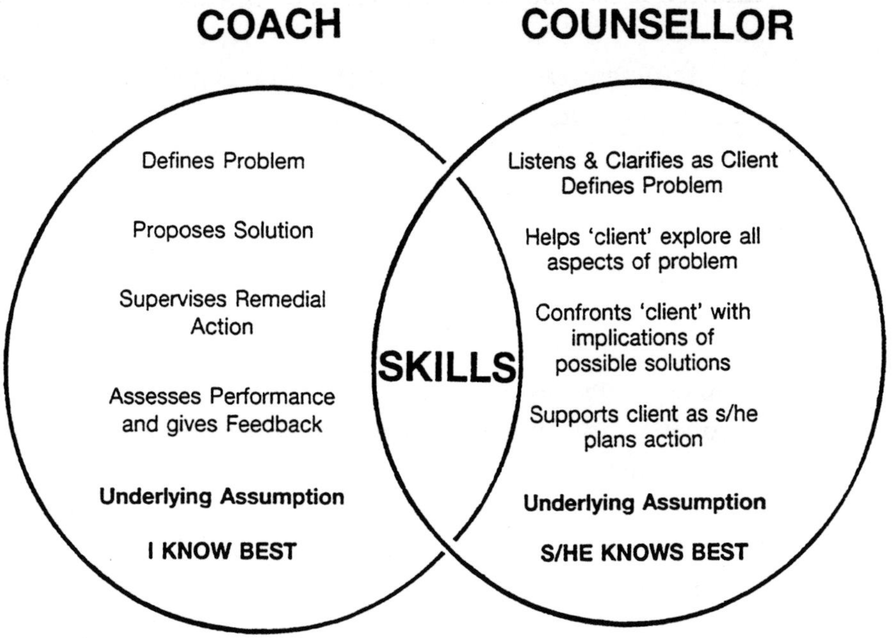

Fig. 4 Coach–Counsellor Actions and Assumptions

The model ignores the possibility, described in the previous chapter, that a coach may involve their 'pupil' in the analysis of what is wrong or what should be done. When coaches do adopt that **style** they begin to use certain techniques and skills of the counsellor. However, most coaches believe 'I know best' and many famous sporting partnerships have broken up when this has been questioned.

Counsellors work hard at getting their 'clients' to face the possible consequences of their plans, but they always accept their right to make their own mistakes. This is perhaps the most significant difference between the mentor and the manager; mentors bear no responsibility for the decisions of their learners, but managers are held accountable for the mistakes of those who report to them.

What do Counsellors Do?

When mentors use counselling skills in order to help someone, the primary focus of their attention is the individual, not the issue they want to help them resolve. Many experienced managers find this hard to remember and often try to understand the problem, when they should be trying to understand the person. Mentors know that the primary focus of their role is the person, so they are less likely to fall into this trap.

Mentors have to suspend judgement, trust the good sense of the other person and have faith in their ability to arrive finally at a sensible decision and sound plan. In other words, they have to respect the person they are counselling and behave in a way which ensures that they are respected and trusted in return. This is particularly important in the latter stages of the counselling process, when the counsellor may need to challenge or confront apparent flaws or contradictions in proposed plans.

Retaining someone's trust, whilst challenging their thinking and, perhaps, causing them to face up to uncomfortable truths about themselves or the situation, is a difficult task. The skills used will be familiar and most of them are used at more than one stage of the process. We will look at the stages first and then look more thoroughly at the skills involved.

Stage 1 **Creating the Climate**

Stage 2 **Exploring and Clarifying the issues**

Stage 3 **Making Decisions and Planning Actions**

Creating the Climate

Chapter 3 stressed the importance of getting the mentor–mentee relationship off to a good start by giving the learner 'high-quality' attention and having them do most of the talking. It also emphasised the importance of cultivating a genuine interest in the learner and demonstrating that this is so.

Mentors will usually have established a relationship based upon mutual respect and trust with their learner, before the need to counsel arises. This, and their use of counselling techniques during their Experiential Learning Cycle discussions, means that most move into the counselling role naturally.

However, it is useful to recognise that anyone who needs counselling is likely to feel vulnerable at some stage of the process, even if they are not to begin with, so respect and trust need to be established at the outset and maintained throughout the session.

Exploring and Clarifying

Counselling is only appropriate when the learner has the capacity to resolve the issue for themselves, but is hampered in doing this by emotional or other difficulties. If they do not have this ability then it is necessary to coach or help them in some other way. On the other hand, provided someone does know how to do something (no matter deeply 'buried' or low their confidence), a skilled counsellor can coach them to competent performance without having any task-related expertise.

Mentors help their protégés to 'step back and open up' the situation troubling them by asking open-ended questions how, when, where, why, etc. They then get learners to explore what they think and feel by reflecting back to them what they appear to have felt, be feeling, saying, or implying and getting them to focus upon what is important to them.

It is particularly helpful if mentors probe for specific concrete detail, so that issues are not examined too superficially. Getting learners to describe the situation from varying viewpoints and to project their thoughts forwards or back in time, helps them to explore what they have felt, and what they want. As a result, mentors can sometimes draw to the learners' attention, changes in their perception or description of the situation they have alluded to, but appear to have ignored.

The mentors' use of counselling skills make it possible for learners, at no risk, to visualise various results and explore possible consequences, so that they feel confident, motivated, and ready to take action. The person being helped has been allowed to move from emotion to rationality at their own pace.

To sum up, allowing someone to attend to a problem or issue by giving them undivided attention and accepting their right to feel as they do, releases their abilities to the full. When the mentor has done all of this (more on the 'how' later), the other person can see their situation more clearly, understand what they want to do about it and is ready to start planning how to achieve this.

Deciding and Acting

Counselling succeeds when the person being helped has a clear plan which they are motivated to put into action. This occurs when they are confident that they have anticipated any likely outcomes or consequences and feel that they have the necessary resources to meet these.

The final task when counselling is to help the other person to formulate concrete, time based, proposals for action. Mentors encourage learners to explore likely outcomes and consequences and to think about how they would feel, and respond to these events if they did occur. During the final stages of planning, mentors can add to learners' confidence and readiness by having them reflect upon the skills, knowledge, experience and aspects of their personality likely to prove of help, and those which might be a hindrance in this situation. Doing this may identify that they need a little extra coaching, or, if they do not, boost their confidence.

The Skills of the Counsellor

The key to the effectiveness of counsellors is that they are trusted. They build this trust because in their dealings with those they help, they are able to show respect, express empathy and demonstrate that they are genuine.

Counsellors show respect when they:

- Ensure privacy and freedom from interruption.
- Listen attentively and actively; giving non-verbal feedback, nodding and smiling appropriately, etc.
- Maintain eye-contact; not staring but always having their eyes available to the speaker.
- Sit in a relaxed, open, non-threatening way; adopting friendly but neutral facial expressions.
- Suspend judgement, and accept the other person's right to feel and think as they do. (The counsellor may need to make them face up to the possible consequences of these feelings and views later in the process.)

Expressing empathy means:

- That mentors have to 'tune-in' to what the other person is feeling, and be prepared to tell the speaker what they see, without any awkwardness or embarrassment.

Demonstrating that they are genuine means:

- being prepared to (briefly) share some of their own experience or difficulties in the area being discussed. (A mentor who talks about similar difficulties they have helped other people resolve, will have the opposite effect as one learner explained to me – they had two thoughts – *'S/he doesn't understand and will s/he talk about me, too, some time?'*) It has to be personal, and represent a matching by the counsellor of the way in which the person being helped has exposed themselves.

Trust stems from this 'mutual vulnerability'. (This is an advantage the mentor has over the line manager. Some managers may be anxious about their status or credibility if they are open in this way – mentors are allowed to be human!) The 'contract' on confidentiality is another source of trust and this means that mentors have to behave at all times as someone who does not gossip and discuss other people's difficulties. It is equally important not to denigrate or criticise others. (It is difficult for someone you are counselling to believe that you will not despise them, if they see you judging the world at large harshly.)

Early in this chapter I hinted that the skills used by counsellors were those of everyday conversation and could be seen regularly in the way that people relate to each other. This is true. The difference lies in the fact that the behaviour of the counsellor is honest, consistent, intentional, well informed and appropriate to the situation. Sadly, not always true in the way people relate to even those they love, on a day-to-day basis.

For example, I once heard a conversation between two 'Cockney' ladies (on the top of a London bus) in which all of these techniques above were used. My eavesdropping started when I heard the words, 'Then 'e swiped me' from one. ' 'e 'it you?' said her friend, suitably shocked (reflecting content). ' 'e tried, but I ducked', came the reply. This clarification is typical of what happens when reflecting and the 'counsellor' followed up with an 'open-ended question'. As I left the bus they were getting to the planning stage, but I doubt if either thought that they had done anything other than have a gossip. The counsellor uses these skills consciously as follows:

Asking Open-ended Questions

These questions which begin How, What, Who, When, Where, Why, get the other person talking and cannot possibly be answered monosyllabically with a 'yes' or 'no'. They are particularly useful in the early stages of the discussion. They have the added merit that they often give the other person some opportunity to influence the direction the discussion takes.

Reflecting

Counsellors use reflection in three main ways. They reflect what people seem to be feeling, their words, the content of what they have said, or sometimes the implied content. They are such a vital tool of counselling that it is worth looking at each of them separately.

Reflecting Feelings

This is probably the most useful, and the technique likely to be used first in a counselling session. Its great strength is that it always leads to greater clarity about the issue being discussed and it helps the speaker to know that the listener really does understand. Frequently it needs to be no more than a word; e.g. 'You feel angry – **sad** – **distressed** – **frustrated** – **confused**'. It is a first class way in which to express empathy and it doesn't seem to matter if you are contradicted – you suggest someone is angry and they will say, *'No, I am disappointed . . .'* and they will tell you why. (This may include an explanation of just why they are angry! – all counsellors have had the experience of clients confirming later something they could not admit/face early on in a session.)

Reflecting Words

This is again a very simple and effective technique which enables a mentor to prompt the person they are helping, without running the risk of the discussion 'going off track'. Early in a session it can 'open up issues', at other times it can help to break through a 'block'. The 'counsellor' listens carefully for emotionally charged words, those given undue emphasis, or for which the speaker's voice fades or becomes barely audible. Simply repeating that one word can have magical effects.

Reflecting Content

This is not a comprehensive summary and it owes nothing to the mentor's brain – it is simple repetition – 'You say that you are not being challenged enough'. It usually results in an elaboration of the point that has been made and provides a way forward directed by the learner. Sometimes it is possible to reflect something which has only been hinted at – the learner cannot quite bring themselves to say it, but they will talk volubly on the subject if the mentor 'legitimises' it for them. I remember once saying, *'You feel we are biased against females here'*. I then sat in total silence for twenty minutes whilst all the evidence and pent-up emotion on this subject was poured out. The dangers with this technique are that you may be suggesting something they do not feel, or give the impression that you think that your statement is true. It should only be used with great discretion and the words *you feel* are important.

Summarising

Mentors are using their own brains at this point, as they reorganise the information they have received, and let the learner know the sense they have made of it.

Confronting

Again, this is a technique which needs to be used with discretion. It may be as simple as pressing for concrete detail from someone who is being vague and unspecific, or it may be pointing out (late in the session), apparent contradictions between what they are saying, and what they said earlier; their body language, how they are saying it; e.g. looking downcast and dropping their voice when they say that something is exciting.

Listening

Mentors, of course, need to listen and these techniques all depend upon careful attention, not only to what is being said, but also how it is said. It is equally important to listen out for what is *not* being said. People who are troubled often start with some subject other than the real problem; (the 'presenting' problem as counsellors call it). This is usually something insoluble and it soon becomes clear that they really want to 'stay on the surface'. Watching as well as listening often provides the first clue.

Summary

As a mentor you can measure your effectiveness as a counsellor; you will never have solved a problem for your learner that s/he was capable of thinking through for themselves. On the other hand, it is important to remember that it is not possible to counsel someone who lacks the necessary skills or knowledge, nor if your relationship is not one of mutual trust and respect.

Counselling is a way of helping someone to identify and overcome what is preventing them from using the relevant skills and knowledge they have. A mentor's behaviour when s/he is not counselling will govern how credible s/he is when s/he does.

Perhaps the last word should go to an experienced mentor: *'One tries not to advise courses of action, but to discuss options, and help the learner towards deciding what is best for them'.*

7

Mentor as Role Model

Introduction

It has been suggested (Chapter 5) that coaching is an area of difficulty for some mentors and being a role model for their learner is controversial for many others. Some people object to the practice of mentoring on these grounds alone. They fear that the primary objective is to turn out 'clones' or 'company men and women'. This can be the first reaction of university graduates. Many have savoured their independence from their parents and feel upon graduation that they are free spirits, well able to make their own way in the world. They need not worry; experienced mentors do not impinge upon the learner's independence, but as one modestly said, *'We are simply people who have probably experienced similar situations in the past'*.

Some new mentors are also uneasy that they are expected to be a 'model' for their learner. The reality is that it is unavoidable. Someone newly appointed to a job or joining an organisation, views any successful and influential person in their orbit as a source of information on how things are done. This chapter will attempt to settle the anxieties new or prospective mentors may have about being part of some 'cloning' exercise and provide more background on role models. Managers reading it may also reflect upon their own style; a significant benefit of the mentor role. As one put it, *'I now feel much more in touch with my own staff. Better able to help with their development and counsel them on career issues'*.

Sometimes the word protégé is used in place of the word learner, and if often causes concern. It seems possible that there is confusion about what the word protégé means, and the footnote on page 26 briefly discusses this issue.

Status apart, formally appointed mentors in any organisation are superior to their protégés. They know and are established in the organisation and probably know the learner's job. This knowledge and experience alone gives them more influence. The significant difference between modern mentors and the Mentor of Greek mythology is that they help to shape the development of adults. The learners have a history of achievement and growth behind them, and are thinking, independent people.

However, as novices within their employing organisation they are, in effect, in a foreign culture with the danger of getting things wrong and perhaps causing offence. It is this 'danger' that makes the mentor role legitimate and worthwhile to both newly appointed employee and employer.

In order to examine why the 'model' role is also appropriate, it is worth thinking more widely about management and the way in which change, growth and development occur in organisations.

Chris Argyris, the industrial psychologist and management consultant and his colleague Donald Schon, have said there is sometimes a difference between the way managers say they manage, and how they actually behave in practice.

A prospective client on a manufacturing site had told me about his organisation, the way in which he managed it and his 'open door' policy, which meant that anyone could approach him at any time, on any issue, on his frequent walks 'on the shop floor', *no matter who he was with.* Later, when we were in the production area, an employee was dismissed with a quick, 'Not now Tom, I've got a visitor'. I am certain that my host did not know that he had done it, but I was interested that it was accepted without any surprise by his employee. It is so easy to say or do something carelessly when we are under pressure or pre-occupied and it is obviously unimportant if it is a temporary lapse and not part of 'who we are and how we operate'. It is our consistent and repeated behaviour which provides the model for those who respect us and may be influenced by us.

The Chief Executive of E.S.B., the Dublin based electricity generating and supply company, not only told his 10,000 employees that training was important and that line management must be involved and committed to it, he gave up nineteen of his Sundays to open a series of management development programmes and then returned to hear each group's final presentations.

Most of us are familiar with what Douglas McGregor called

'Theory X' and 'Theory Y' approaches to management. He said that some people behave as if they believed that the only way to get results was to give precise directions, closely supervise, and cajole or scold those who worked for them (Theory X). Others, he said, seemed to regard work as natural as play and to believe that people had an innate desire to perform well. These managers simply set goals clearly, agreed standards of performance, reviewed progress periodically and were available for help if required. McGregor called them 'Theory Y' managers. Most importantly, he asserted that these 'theories' were self-fulfilling prophecies; both sets of managers experienced the behaviour that they expected.

Argyris' point is that many managers talk as if they are 'Theory Y' managers, but behave as if their beliefs are in line with 'Theory X'. Their 'espoused theory' should cause them to relate to staff as mature, responsible, highly-motivated individuals, but their 'theory in use' results in them treating people as if they were irresponsible children. This is important, because the way in which people are managed appears to have a significant effect upon how they behave, develop, and in time, manage others. An enormous amount was written about 'company culture' during the 1980s and many organisations are devoting great resources to changing their operating culture in order to cope with the expected challenges of the 21st century.

At the risk of over simplifying I believe that this effort can be summed up as an attempt to do three things:

- Change the way in which people feel about themselves; increasing their sense of personal power and therefore their willingness to take more initiative.

- Change the way in which manager and managed relate so that organisations can be 'flatter' – less hierarchical and therefore able to communicate more effectively and respond more rapidly to change and other challenges.

- Change the way in which people think about their organisation and the environment in which it operates.

Increasingly, employees are being asked to break out of their old 'mind-sets'; to find new paradigms or models of how their organisation and the 'world' may look. There is much talk of 'customer driven' and 'strategic alliances' to supplement the old preoccupations with competitive analysis and vertical integration, etc.

Many attempts to change the way a department or organisation functions, founder because management are not 'walking the way they talk'. Managers say that principles, practices, procedures or values have to change, but employees recognise that they are still paying attention to the same aspects of performance and rewarding or punishing in the same way.

It can sometimes be difficult for an individual manager to be entirely consistent. As a production supervisor in a tyre company I had to insist upon a certain procedure which was not difficult for the tall, slim, young, recently recruited operatives. Unfortunately, other operators who were middle-aged, less than 5′6″ in height and with more than twenty years' service, could not 'press the button and wind the handle at the same time' as instructed. Their arms were too short to reach and they were not strong enough in any case. They had developed their own improvisation and all supervisors 'turned a blind eye' to this practice knowing that they, the supervisors, would be rebuked whenever the production manager saw the malpractice upon his walks through the workshop. The real problem was a lack of consultation with experienced employees during the recently completed modernisation of the production line – which is another story and one not likely to happen today.

The importance of this to you if you are a mentor, is that all human beings seem to set greater store by what they see happening, than by what is said to them. Your way of relating to your learner and the way s/he sees you relating to staff and colleagues, will make much more impression than anything you say. Your effectiveness in managing your time together and the way in which you prepare for meetings, delegating appropriately, so that you are not interrupted, will say volumes about you and what you believe to be important. If your learner has the misfortune to be poorly managed, you need never criticise, nor collude with them in any way. Your maturity in helping them to think through how to address the issue, and what you say about your own staff, colleagues, your boss and the company in the process, will clearly indicate what you believe is right and wrong.

Summary

It is not the mentor's role to turn a learner into a company 'clone' or someone cast in their own image (even if it is their perception that this would enormously enhance everyone's working life!). It is more important that mentors, by their behaviour, provide a standard against which the new employee, or job-holder can form a sound judgement of how they want to go about seeking success in their own career.

A number of mentors have said that being free of responsibility for their learner's performance at work, makes it easier for them to be consistent in work and deed. As one explained, *'My time with my learner is "planned time" – I am never under pressure or shooting from the hip'*. To the new employee in particular, the mentor and their boss are the company, and represent models of success. What mentors do is ten times more powerful than what they say and it shows. One learner remarked, *'I was always impressed by my mentor. She always seemed to have time for me even though she was very busy, and she seemed the same with her staff too'*.

8

How Will it All End?

Introduction

Both mentors and their learners, particularly in the early stages of a formal mentoring relationship, express concern about how and when it will end. Learners who do not yet appreciate the relationship, or value the contribution it can make to their development and future career, can feel that it is an 'apprenticeship' which has to be endured. Mentors, with other demands on their time, do want to help but can feel that they need to know when the commitment will end.

It is impossible to say categorically how long a mentor–protégé relationship will last; some informal relationships last a lifetime. Organisations with formal schemes which prescribe a specific length of time, find that some people keep in touch for years whilst others reach a 'natural end' before the full period has expired. It is equally impossible to provide mentors with specific guidelines for their final 'official' meeting, because by then the relationship has become unique to them and the learner. What we can say is that changes will have occurred in the learner's self-confidence and perception of themselves. This seems to be equally true for both new recruits and those with substantial work experience, who have been mentored through an internal job change. It is also likely that as they developed, they experienced a specific set of mood and behaviour changes. This chapter will discuss these changes and the stages most mentoring relationships go through.

For the sake of simplicity I will first describe the stages of change in a general way and then mention ways in which mentors use this model. Mentors surveyed two and three years after initial training described what follows, as not only making great sense to them personally, but also helping them *'to understand and be tolerant of my learner when things got difficult'*. A typical reaction from someone who was also a manager was: *'it helped to know where someone was . . . I never bother with the theory, it just helps me to manage myself.'*

These changes were first observed in people coping with bereavement and confirmed by subsequent research involving people experiencing other changes.

Stage 1 – Immobilisation

People appear not to believe what has happened. They cannot think about the consequences or make any immediate plans or decisions. They need time to let the news sink in. Even very good news, like a better than expected examination result, is doubted and the person may go to some lengths to get 'independent' confirmation. Bad news is often greeted with an apparent lack of emotion; almost as if both thinking and feeling systems shut down in order to protect the person from too much pain.

Stage 2 – Minimisation

In this subtle change the 'thinking system' seems to collude in keeping the person from facing reality. They may deny that a change has taken place, or declare that it will not effect them much. Positive statements about sad events; *'It was a nice way to go'*, or, *'At least she is out of pain now'*, are common. Even exciting events are minimised, as if people want to protect themselves from pain if subsequently something goes wrong.

Stage 3 – Depression

At the third stage, people really begin to face the reality of what has happened; to think about what life is going to be like without a loved one, or a job which has been enjoyed. Some experience feelings of helplessness or anger at the way in which 'fate' has treated them. Those promoted or accepted by a university may experience anxiety about their ability to cope. The speed with which people reach this stage, the depth and length of any depression, varies enormously with the nature of the event and the individual's personality. However, even the most exciting of events in life seems to have their short downturn in optimism and elation.

Stage 4 – Letting Go

Stage 4 is vital in dealing successfully with change and coming through a transition a more capable, mature or nicer person. People are putting the past behind them. Someone who has lost a partner accepts that they are not coming back. The redundant or retired person realises that they can no longer think of themselves as . . . . . Those promoted leave behind some work companions or, perhaps, a particular way of thinking about themselves.

Stage 5 – Testing Out

The more dramatic the change being experienced, the more clearly this phase will be recognised. A new repertoire of behaviours or set of beliefs may be 'tried', to see how they fit. The past is being left behind; experiments with being the 'new' person have begun. Divorced people may change hair styles, dress, car and perhaps even moral standards. Newly appointed managers may swing from *laissez-faire* to a strongly directing style, as they seek ways of managing which suit them. People are learning and developing as they come to grips with the change.

Stage 6 – Searching for Meaning

At this point people are beginning to emerge from the transition and to make sense of the way in which their lives are different. They may make decisions about which of their 'experimental' behaviours do suit them. They stand back and take stock; a time of insights, hindsight and perhaps, some rationalisation of their 'testing out', period.

Stage 7 – Internalisation

This final stage is self explanatory; the change has become part of the person and they have become part of the change. They may have added to their repertoire of behaviours and skills, changed their beliefs or values or

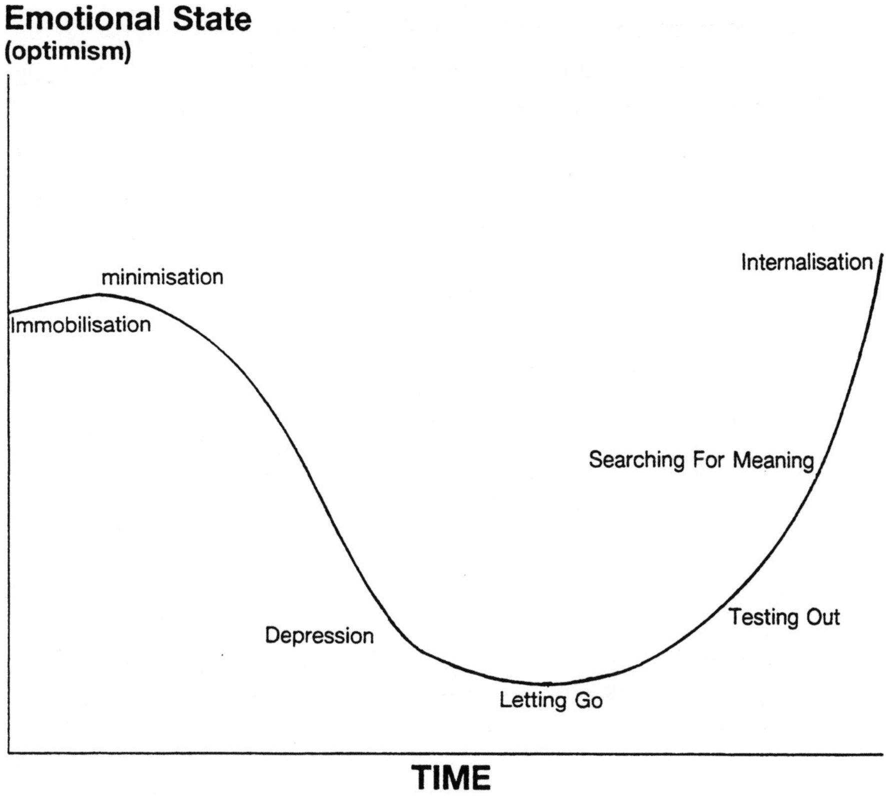

Fig. 5 Transitions

simply see themselves as being 'older and wiser'; having a better understanding of things they thought they knew before.

Summary

Although these stages were described as generalisations, there does seem to be evidence that all people undergoing change, which is likely to have an impact upon how they live their life, go through the transition cycle above. What does vary is the length of time people take to go through the entire cycle and the extent to which they are aware of, or devote energy to, any particular stage. The stages are not discrete and it is not unknown for someone to devote a lot of energy to *'testing out'* before they have *'let go'* and to find themselves dragged back down into depression, when they thought that they had begun to adjust and had put the past behind them.

It is not suggested that mentors should attempt to be amateur psychologists, but it is worth recalling this cycle when faced with a learner who is performing below expectations or required standards. What life events have they had to cope with recently? Is their behaviour consistent with any particular phase of the transition cycle? At one level mentor–learner relationships are one long transition and it is worth considering the changes they may go through.

Stages of the Mentoring Relationship

As a mentor, your relationship with your learner is not analogous to that of parent and child, but it is a good point of comparison. The parent–child relationship moves from total dependence, to total independence in approximately twenty years. Sensible parents do not expect gratitude. They are content with their memories and to have children who are ready for adult life. Parents who *'let go'* and achieve this frame of mind, probably see more of their offspring and have a better, more mature relationship with them, than those who do not.

Learners are never totally dependent on mentors. From the

outset mentors have tried to treat them as equals, despite their lack of experience and differences in age or status at work. Like parents, mentors should not to expect gratitude from learners, but recognise that this relationship will also change over time.

Early Stages – Resistance and Dependence

The early mentor–learner relationship is tentative and polite, as each person *'feels the other out'* and decides what level of trust and friendship is possible. Learners may have a natural desire to prove themselves self-sufficient; some may declare that they do not need a mentor. This early, difficult phase may give way to a slightly dependent need for approval. This can result in stilted conversations and mentors may sense resistance to a view they are expressing, which does not surface. They are not openly challenged as they might expect.

Middle Stage – A Meeting of Equals

Once the relationship is firmly established, many mentors find that they derive considerable benefit and stimulation from it. If they are also managers, the *'safe'* climate created means that mentors sometimes hear points of view and information that their staff withhold. Learners still receive the benefit of years of experience and knowledge of the organisation, but this 'meeting' of equals is reported to result in lively debates which cause mentors to re-examine cherished beliefs and practices.

Final Stage – Social or As Required

Towards the end of their time with a particular learner, mentors find that it has become a much more social relationship, because there is less on the 'agenda' to discuss. Alternatively, meetings become less regular. The likelihood is that the final meeting, and subsequent relationship, will be a natural development of what has occurred over the mentoring period. Some want to keep in touch with each other, but there is no obligation to do so and the mentor's wishes are as valid as the learner's at this point.

Summary

In most cases, formal mentoring starts out as difficult and artificial, but grows into a real and mutually valued relationship. As the most senior and experienced person involved, mentors take responsibility for this development. In doing so they will have used the coaching, counselling, and other techniques in this book sensitively and honestly. Good mentors will have regularly reviewed how well the relationship was working and encouraged an open dialogue with their learner on what each has done that has been helpful, and what, if anything, has been getting in the way. Many mentors say that the experience has given them personal learning, satisfaction and enjoyment. I wish you the same.

A fuller account of the theory of transitions and some of the research which underpins it can be found in Chapter 10 of *Psychology and Management – a text for managers and trade unionists,* edited by Cary L Cooper and published by Macmillan (1981).

9

Can It Go Wrong?

Introduction

The focus in this book so far has been on 'what to do and how to do it', if you are a mentor. There have also been references to coping with difficulties like handling learners who are unaware of their deficiencies, or insensitive to the impact of their behaviour on others. However, there are a good many other aspects of mentoring which can go wrong. This chapter will briefly describe some of these and the steps taken to overcome them by organisations with formal mentoring schemes.

Life is never simple when we are dealing with human beings and neither people nor problems can be put into neat boxes. Despite this fact, I shall group the difficulties I have encountered and had reported to me in surveys, under the headings of personality, gender, training support, 'life events' and administration.

Personality

Not everyone is suited to the role of mentor and some learners can also be difficult to help by this method, because they resist requirements placed upon them like keeping a record of their experience and discussing it with their mentor. They may lack ability at the **Examine and Reflect** stage of the 'learning from experience cycle' (Chapter 2), or perhaps be prejudiced against learning anything except through books, lectures and other conventional methods.

The personality of the mentor is a critical factor in the success of any mentoring relationship. To mentor informally there must be a genuine interest in the learner and it seems likely that this is done by people who are generally interested in and keen to help others.

In one organisation employing a high proportion of very highly qualified scientists, this was a major problem. Recruited from academic institutions after several years of post-graduate study and research, they were totally devoted to their specialism to the exclusion of almost everything else. Their work was their pleasure and few had any outside interests. At the extreme of this group was the mentor whose learner said of him, *'Talking with him was like drawing teeth, he just seemed incredibly shy'*. A number of other mentors in this group were at ease when discussing work-related 'technical' issues, but as another learner said, *'She was great in helping me think problems through but I could never imagine raising a personal issue. She'd freak. My boss was better'*. They may have been wrong, we will never know, but it was the perception which influenced the learner's behaviour. A number of 'unsuitable' mentors had volunteered believing it to be 'a good career move' because of the seniority and personality of the scheme's sponsor.

These mentors received two days of training which included a self-score personality questionnaire. This helped to highlight the traits of which certain prospective mentors needed to be aware and compensate for, when relating to others. It is interesting to note that the first questionnaire chosen (used by some companies in selecting staff), could not discriminate between the initial group of mentors; they all came out with same personality profile.

It is important that prospective mentors know that although there are personal benefits to be gained from their involvement in the scheme, it will not adversely affect their careers if they decline. The ideal is an effective means of self-selection. One company carried out a 'tough-minded counselling' session with each volunteer after the training had been completed, in which they thoroughly explored their suitability for the role before finally committing themselves. Other organisations (e.g. 'Role Model' example Chapter 1), base selection upon information received from the volunteers or those they work for.

Training too, is important but it must be recognised that this can only help someone who wants to develop skills which do not come naturally to them; a short training experience cannot change anything as fundamental as personality.

The personality of the learner is less often a problem because the mentoring scheme is usually part of a 'contract' they have entered into in joining an organisation or accepting a particular job. There are, of course, personality clashes and mentors have asked for help because they 'just don't like their learner'. This is often a temporary feeling which goes when mentors are encouraged to re-visit the information on 'Transitions' (Chapter 8), reminded that the purpose of their role is not to produce a 'clone' and are given help in identifying whether the difficulty is a suitable subject for coaching or counselling. In one case the relationship went on to last far beyond the official mentoring period. This mentor remarked, *'I think that we **both** matured a lot in that first twelve months'*.

On the other hand some relationships will break down or prove unsuitable and there does need to be a 'safety valve', which enables people to receive help or change the situation in which they find themselves. Sometimes this is a human resources department function, other organisations have a sponsor or nominated person to whom either mentor or learner can turn. This works best if there is some form of regular, even informal contact, with those involved as mentors and learners. Raising the subject of difficulty in a mentoring relationship is not easy because it is bound to feel, by either party, a failure or defeat.

Gender

The issues aroused by cross-gender mentoring cannot be ignored. My experience suggests that, where it is possible, better results are obtained when females, in particular, are mentored by someone of their own sex. There is a more natural bond, discussion of a wider range of topics is made easier and the power of the role model is greater. Until recently, the 'sponsor' model could only work on a cross-gender basis for females, but this is improving as more of them rise to senior positions and are available as mentors. Other problems associated with cross-gender mentoring are also diminishing as males become more conscious of their own behaviour and more females acquire an easy assertiveness. There does seem to be some 'cultural' advantage in males being mentored by females as one young man said, *'Having had . . . as my mentor I would never have any anxiety about reporting to a woman'*. Just as well, as he is very likely to have that experience during his career.

Training Support

Many of the problems in this area are due to a failure to recognise the complexity of the mentor's role. Whatever approach is adopted (Chapter 1), a good mentor combines the skills and qualities of a parent, manager, and friend in a unique blend but the fact that a prospective mentor has been all three, does not usually mean that a quick half-day briefing is sufficient for them to be truly competent.

Learners, too, derive more from the relationship if they are trained. If the process of self-knowledge, appreciation of how we learn from experience and the development of their personal network takes place before the first formal review with their mentor, then problems are minimised and learning receives a boost.

Training alone is not enough and the wise organisation 'protects its investment' in mentoring by providing a coordinator to monitor its success and support those involved at a personal level and through periodic meetings of mentors, learners and sometimes both.

Life Events

Professional counsellors will not 'work' with someone on an issue they have not resolved themselves. This is because they know that if they are having to cope with bereavement or the break-up of a relationship themselves, they may not be able to give their undivided attention to someone who is troubled in these areas. In a similar way someone having taken on a mentoring responsibility may have so much happening in their own life that they have no 'space' for helping others. It may be that an event is 'too close to home'.

One learner experienced this. Talking about his mentor he said, *'He suddenly went berserk, calling me irresponsible and immoral. I thought that he was going to have a heart attack or something'*. It emerged that the young man was talking about the difficulties he was having with his fianceé's parents because she had decided to set up home with him before their marriage. The mentor was currently suffering distress because his daughter was doing the same, despite the disapproval of himself and his wife.

Obviously the 'neutral ear' of the mentor was not available and other help was required. The coordinator mentioned above, or another member of the mentor network (Chapter 4), would have been ideal. Training can help mentors recognise these situations and help them to cope with the moral or ethical dilemmas they cause, but an 'outside' resource is probably best.

Administration

The reader will have noticed that the divisions used in this chapter are arbitrary and a number of the examples given overlap the categories chosen. Life is like that and mentoring is no different. Whether you are an informal mentor to someone you chose, or who requested your help, or part of some corporate initiative your employer has taken, your experience as a mentor will be unique; it will not fit neatly into a box chosen by me to make communication easier.

That said, there are certain ways of setting up and managing formal mentoring schemes which seem to increase the chance that they will succeed. These are:

Communicate and Communicate Again

- Explain to line managers and other employees why the scheme is being set up and what it is designed to achieve.

- Remind 'bosses' when 'mentored' staff are joining them, about their responsibility for explaining to them how the scheme operates and how it fits in with other staff development activities.

- Ensure that mentors thoroughly understand their role and their responsibility for explaining to their learners how the scheme is going to work for them and what other developmental support is available.

- Make it clear whether the mentor, boss or learner has the primary responsibility for arranging the first meeting.

Coordinate

- The first meeting between all learners and their mentors and have some mechanism for identifying quickly any lapse in mentors and learners meeting promptly.

One approach is to mount a 'social' event like a lunch or after-hours 'cheese and wine party', at which a check is made that every one has met their 'partner' and arranged the time and place of the first meeting.

Monitor

- Check the development of the relationships by regular reviews (2–3 per year minimum), with both mentors and learners.

- Evaluate the success of the scheme by carrying out an audit every year or two periodically using an outsider to design questionnaires and conduct in-depth interviews.

Remain Flexible and Integrate

- Be prepared to extend the group to whom mentoring is available.

- Always ensure that the mentor programme is integrated with mainstream staff development activities.

Mentoring can easily be seen as some form of exclusive club with all the difficulties and envy that implies. Much of the training that mentors receive has a wider application and the more thoroughly the skills and values of mentoring permeate an organisation's culture, the more likely it is that it will be come a 'learning organisation' which can respond rapidly to change and be flexible to customer needs.

Summary

Mentoring is not a panacea nor is it a way of getting training 'done on the cheap'. It is an approach to liberating and empowering employees which can benefit the mentor almost as much as the learner. It is an ideal way of supporting 'culture change' efforts if mentors are appropriately selected and trained. Finally it is an approach to encouraging people to grow to their full potential, which may be as old as history but is entirely consistent with the most up-to-date thinking in managing and learning.

Bibliography

Readers will probably recognise that this book is firmly rooted in practical experience rather than theory. No further reading is required; it provides the insights and knowledge necessary to build upon your natural skills and experience in order to become a competent mentor. Those who do want to read more on any aspect of the topics covered will find that the following provide both a good starting point and references to further reading.

Everyone Needs a Mentor, David Clutterbuck (IPM 1991)
This 2nd edition is much more comprehensive than the 1985 original although only 21 pages longer. It provides a good overview of the subject and is likely to be found invaluable to anyone introducing a mentoring programme.

Networking & Mentoring, Dr Lily M. Segerman-Peck (Piatkus 1991)
The author's experience as a mentor shines through this

book. It is sub-titled *'A Woman's Guide'* but could help mentors of either sex. It will also be useful to learners who want to seek a mentor or derive the maximum benefit from the one they have.

I'm OK – You're OK, Thomas Harris MD (Pan 1973)
Originally published in 1967 this book is probably still the best introduction to Transactional Analysis (TA) written. Despite its obscure name TA is straightforward, practical, and can provide important insights into the way in which we relate to and manage others; effective mentors use TA even if they do not know the theory.

Counselling people at work, Robert de Board (Gower 1983)
Formerly a lecturer at the Henley Management College, Bob writes clearly about the kinds of situations managers may face when counselling staff.

The Skilled Helper, Gerard Egan (Calif. Brooks/Cole 1975)
This book is highly regarded by professional counsellors and Egan's work forms the basis of many other books on this subject.

Assertiveness at Work, Ken and Kate Back (McGraw-Hill (UK) 1982)
An excellent book on this important subject. People who have attended training programmes on Assertion in the UK and elsewhere will recognise its influence.

Psychology and Management, Ed. Cary L. Cooper (Macmillan Press 1981)
A good general text with contributions from many first class writers on Counselling, Stress, Transitions and other related subjects.

Passages, Gail Sheehy (Bantam Books 1982)
An easy to read account which describes the problems and issues which people face at various stages of their lives and careers.

Managing Your Own Career, Dave Francis (Fontana/ Collins 1985)
Illustrated with lots of 'case histories' and full of useful questionnaires, it is stimulating and practical.

The Origins and Growth of Action Learning, R.W. Revans (Chartwell-Bratt Bromley & Lund 1982)

Other Sources

Although this book was written for practical people rather than theoreticians it has been said that *'There is nothing so practical as a good theory'* and some people may like to read the books specifically mentioned in the text or some of the others which have influenced what has been written. The following short alphabetical (by Author) list makes no distinctions – all are worth reading.

Argyris & Schon, *The Reflective Practitioner*, Addison Wesley, 1978

Argyris & Schon, *Theory in Practice,* Jossey Bass, 1974

Boyatzis, Richard E., *The Competent Manager,* John Wiley & Sons, 1982

Cameron-Bandler, L,, Gordon, D. and Lebeau, M., *The Emprint Method,* FuturePace Inc 1985

Covey, Stephen, R., *The 7 Habits of Highly Effective People,* Simon & Schuster, 1989

Grove, Andrew S., *High Output Management,* Random House, 1983

Hunt, John, *Managing People at Work,* Pan Books, 1981

Kanter, Rosabeth Moss, *The Change Masters*, Unwin Paperbacks, 1985

Kolb, D.A., Rubin, I.M. and McIntyre, J.M., *Organizational Psychology*, Prentice-Hall, 1979

McGregor, Douglas, *The Human Side of Enterprise*, McGraw-Hill, 1960

Plant, Roger, *Managing Change and Making it stick*, Fontana Collins, 1987

Pedler, M., Burgoyne, J. and Boydell T., *A Manager's Guide to Self-Development*, McGraw-Hill, 1978

Pedler et al., *The Learning Company*, McGraw-Hill, 1991

Schein, Edgar H., *Career Dynamics*, Addison Wesley, 1978

Tiffin, J. & McCormick, E.J. *Industrial Psychology*, George Allen & Unwin, 1965